Praise for Cour~~~ ~~
Meghan biograp
3) and

"Love how intellige ....~~ books are. [Hargrove] is factual, fair, sees both sides and has a wonderful sense of humor. Can't wait for the next book." —**Amazon reviewer**

"I couldn't put this book down. I fell asleep to it." —**Goodreads reviewer**

"Filled with information that I did not know about royalty. Just a great read. Prepare to be amazed. Be careful of the wow factor in this book." —**Amazon reviewer**

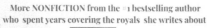

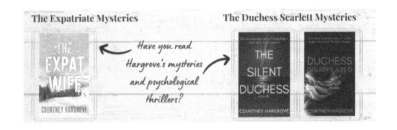

"An unputdownable psychological thriller that'll have you reading long into the night. I loved this book—the dynamics between the characters makes this an addictive read." —BookGirlBrown_Reviews

Hargrove is a master at keeping us as confused and questioning as her protagonist…[she keeps us in suspense for over 300 pages…you know why Courtney Hargrove is a number one best-selling author." —Readers' Favorite book reviews

Harry & Meghan

Vol. 4: The Great Jam Wars

Courtney Hargrove

One Moment Books

Published by ONE MOMENT BOOKS

For information, address
OneMomentBooks@Outlook.com

Dear Reader,

Sorry I'm late.

Or, as Reese Witherspoon encourages women to say instead, thank you for waiting.

Friends of this Sussex biography series have come to expect a new volume every summer. I cover the life and times of Harry, Meghan, Lilibet and Archie, Pula and Guy (rest in peace, sweet boy; that's news for the next volume) over a twelve-month cycle from summer to summer, and this edition will continue that tradition despite its unusual publication date.

So, although this was published in March 2025, it picks up where Volume 3 left off, which means it covers Prince Harry and Duchess Meghan's lives from August 2023 through July 2024.

Things were going well with Volume 4 at first. I began writing this book when I was supposed to, in the autumn of 2023.

But life surprised me in the midst of executing my plans for the year, and I retreated.

The scary news was in November, and the biopsy was in January 2024. The results came in February. The surgeon's recommendation for a full thyroid removal was in March. April was for driving across state lines for a second opinion at a world-class cancer hospital. Summer was for worrying. September was for the operation and coming to terms with a new me in the mirror, now with a permanent slash across my throat, like I'd been knifed in a dark alley. Winter was for healing. It was interesting how in certain ways my medical experience over those months was parallelling what we were being told about a princess who still lives in Britain.

I ended up behind in everything I'd wanted to excel at in a year: Work, finances, fitness, friendships, reading, writing. I felt like a somnolent failure, stagnating when everyone else was moving forward.

I came across the writing of Donna Ashworth at just the right time. I often re-read this meditation when I need a reminder to go easy on myself (you'll find the full passage in her book *Life: Poems to help navigate life's many twists & turns,* and on social media). I hope you can all be kind and forgiving to yourselves in this time of turmoil and uncertainty. You are not lazy and you are not weak and you are not lacking. In fact, Ashworth writes,

…Your bone composition matches the coral in the seas and you, my friend, are ruled by the moon and the sun. Whether you like it or not. So no, you are not lazy…Nature is simply pulling you to slow, like the life, floral and fauna around you. It is not your moment to rise. It is winter, you are wintering. And you are right on time.

As always, thank you for reading and for coming along on this journey chronicling the lives of the Duke and Duchess of Sussex and their family.

If you're new to my work, I'm a reporter who covered the royal family—among many other assignments—for *People* magazine for years. I had the chance to interview Meghan around 2015-ish but back then, editors of big publications didn't find her famous enough to write much about, so I turned her down...and yes, I count this as one of my (minor) regrets in life.

I chronicle each year in the life of Harry and Meghan through storytelling, rigorous research to ensure truth and accuracy, transparency, and a strong dose of humor.

Once again, I find myself asking, where did *another* year go? One minute it's 2020 and Harry and Meghan are making an historic break from Britain's royal family, and the next they're blending into American Independence Day celebrations, Meghan's building a new brand, and I'm publishing Volume 4 of their American life.

Now, let's dive in.

xoCourtney

"There are many different things to eat and they taste many different ways. But when I have bread and jam I always know what I am getting, and I am always pleased."

—*Bread and Jam for Frances*, by Russell Hoban
Lilian Hoban

Contents

Prologue

On December 28, 2023, a procession of vehicles, lights flashing, cruised down a darkened street in central London. The dramatic convoy included a shiny black sedan, police cars with lights on, cops on motorcycles, and a selection of Range Rovers, some marked, some not.

There was clearly a VIP a on the move—but *who was it?* And why was the heavily protected sedan heading straight toward Harley Street, an area of Britain's capital city known for its medical practices and hospitals?

Witnesses knew there was a finite number of bigwigs who would be granted such close protection, both private and taxpayer funded. *Who would require such a robust procession in those quiet days just after Christmas?*

Indeed, the fact that all of this was occurring in the small space between holidays, a time when Europe and the UK go quiet, those lost days between December 25 and January 1 when we barely know what day it is, raised questions with witnesses who suspected the precious cargo might be a member of the British royal family. Everyone knows Range Rovers and Land Rovers are the royals' signature brand, after all.

Wrote one royal watcher on Twitter, where a video of the vehicles taking up a major London street was posted, "I hope all is well at Sandringham."

The implication in that Tweet, of course, was that the person being escorted by law enforcement had been rushed to London from Sandringham, the grand estate in Norfolk, England, where King Charles III and select family members were celebrating Christmas.

Could the convoy *really* have been for a senior royal? If it was, this would signal something was terribly wrong with one of them. The family famously spends both big holidays at Sandringham. As their official website explains,

The Royal Family traditionally spends Christmas and New Year at Sandringham House. [sic] The Queen's country estate in Norfolk. During the sixties, when Her Majesty's children were small, many Christmases were celebrated at Windsor Castle, where The Royal Family spends Easter. But since 1988, when the castle was being rewired, Royal Christmases returned to Sandringham.

In any case, the convoy rolled on, and no one was any wiser about whether there was a senior royal in that car and, if so, what might be wrong.

With that, things went utterly off the rails with the British royal family as the world watched. The family would soon be under extreme scrutiny, with concern and speculation that would grow louder with each passing day, running wild with no end in sight.

Many would wonder: Was the institution of the British monarchy crumbling before our eyes?

With Prince Harry and Duchess Meghan living in California and unburdened of their positions as working royals, you'd think they could quietly live their lives from afar, with private notes and messages sent across the pond to offer support during the crisis that was to come.

In that case, perhaps everything that happened with the British royals in the first months of 2024 would have no place in a Sussex biography.

But it took them—"them" being tabloids and anonymous "royal sources" worldwide—mere days to make the unprecedented royal drama about Meghan and the Sussexes, and therefore everything that happened after that December 28 convoy is germane to the topic I've written about for several years now, that of Prince Harry and Duchess Meghan.

That year would be a mess of epic proportions, and we shall cover it in all its gory detail.

PART I:

The Calm Before the Storm

Chapter 1

August 2023

The dog days of summer brought dry, hot winds and the Pacific's gently lapping waves to Montecito, perfect conditions for Prince Harry and Duchess Meghan to build sandcastles with their children and play fetch with their black Labrador, Pula.

Unfortunately, things weren't 100 percent peaceful *inside* the walls of the House of Sussex. Harry and Meghan were still reeling from a messy public breakup that made news weeks before, which in turn was accompanied by a barrage of negative press and brutal headlines.

As readers of Volume 3 of this series will recall, a shocking report emerged in the summer of 2023 that claimed Spotify, a top streaming service for content creators, was severing ties with Harry and Meghan, putting the kibosh on a blockbuster, high-dollar partnership.

The *Wall Street Journal's* scoop said the couple had not met productivity "benchmarks" that Spotify expected, and therefore would not collect an estimated payout of around $20 million (a figure that was never confirmed). Never mind that Meghan's Spotify podcast, *Archetypes*, had won multiple awards, including a Gracie Award for top entertainment podcast host. It wasn't enough to keep the partnership afloat.

Meghan and Harry's team scrambled. William Morris Endeavor, the agency that reps Meghan, released a statement insisting the split was mutual, but even so, it was clear this was not news the couple was ready to share. The floodgates opened within the previously soft-on-the-Sussexes U.S.-based media, and even upmarket and credible publications now aimed their barbs at the Sussexes without mercy.

Ugly adjectives hurled at them by the *Journal*, *Rolling Stone* and the *Guardian* newspaper, for example, included "flop," "grifters," "trainwreck" and "no-talent."

Harry and Meghan, now tightly woven into the fabric of their exclusive Santa Barbara community of Montecito, didn't publicly show the strain. Their home offices and twin "thrones," as one reporter described their seats next to one another in the space they share when it's time to work, was where they privately dealt with the fresh challenges coming their way.

There was also some feeling that much of this was out of their control, and there was no sense wringing their hands about things they couldn't change.

They couldn't change the fact that their names were clickbait and cash flow for the lowest forms of tabloid scum. The big "news" organizations didn't actually need fresh news anymore to create content—opinions, guesses and lies did the trick nicely.

Harry and Meghan kept their heads down.

They did the work.

In the first week of August, Meghan and Harry's team cut through the noise about their failures to provide fresh content like a laser.

The Duke and Duchess of Sussex's own company, Archewell Productions, had bought the rights to the *New York Times* bestselling novel *Meet Me at the Lake*—a runaway hit with a built-in fan base—from Penguin Random House, one of the major publishing houses in the U.S.

And in late summer of 2023, we learned Meghan and Harry would collaborate with Netflix to bring the story from the page to the screen. In announcing this move, they lobbed another hit against false reports that the streaming behemoth was through with the Sussexes. Netflix wasn't done working with them. Not by a longshot.

What was interesting about that announcement, besides the fact it branded Archewell as a player in the film production space, was the choice of story. One could almost see the outline of Meghan and Harry in *Meet Me at the Lake*, though of course some of the details are different.

The protagonists, Will and Fern, meet in their twenties and fall in love instantly. They make a plan to meet up one year later, but devastatingly to Fern, Will never shows up. It's not all over for them, though: A decade later, it becomes clear the couple still has a chance. Indeed, *Meet Me at the Lake* hits narrative points that mimic the Sussexes' own lives. One character loses a parent in a car crash, as Harry did. Another experiences postpartum struggles. And it all takes place in or around Toronto, where Meghan lived while shooting *Suits*.

It looked like a great fit, and once again, the wheels turned behind the scenes while those rooting against them waited for failure that still hadn't come.

Meanwhile, on the heels of that fun news, the palace back in England got petty.

And I mean…*petty*. Buckingham Palace, which is also the office of King Charles III, had a choice to make.

It all started on one presumably slow news day, when a reporter with the British tabloid the *Express* poked around the royal family's official website, Royal.uk, and found some irregularities.

To wit: Queen Elizabeth II had died a year before, but according to the Royal Family's official website, she was still the reigning monarch of Great Britain. You'd be forgiven for scratching your head and checking your calendar if you saw the *74-plus mentions* of QEII being the monarch in the year 2023 when she was long dead and buried.

If those embarrassing errors weren't bad enough, in eight places on the royal family's official website, King Charles was titled as the Prince of Wales while his queen wife, Camilla, was listed as the Duchess of Cornwall four times. Prince Harry was referred to as His Royal Highness, which the *Express* helpfully reminded us was incorrect because of the "Megxit" agreement of 2020 removing the HRH from Harry's title.

As readers of this series will recall, the palace's official statement in January of that year left no doubt about Harry's new status: "The Sussexes will not use their HRH titles as they are no longer working members of the Royal Family."

But for more than three years, the family's official website referred to Harry as HRH.

That still doesn't cover all the errors. The newspaper went on to point out that "Prince William and Kate are also called the Duke and Duchess of Cambridge three times. While this is technically correct, as William and Kate do still hold these titles, they became the Prince and Princess of Wales last September and are now primarily referred to as this, as is reflected in their updated individual pages on the website."

In all, the *Express* said they found "Eighteen pages across the leading website, which promises 'to provide an authoritative resource of information,' [to be] factually wrong."

Why am I subjecting you to a laundry list of royal inefficiencies? Stay with me.

The Express reported this information on a Friday.

By Tuesday, a few fixes were made to the official website. The palace had a choice, and their first correction was about *one particular* royal.

Buckingham Palace, it seemed, sent down orders that certain facts must be *swiftly* corrected.

Can you guess—can you stretch that brilliant mind of yours and take a *wild guess*—which mistakes were fixed first? Which errors were deemed most offensive and were corrected with great speed?

Congratulations! Because I know you got it. Prince Harry's HRH title was scrubbed without delay.

"The Duke was twice referred to as His Royal Highness (HRH) on his profile page, but after the *Express* reported the error on Friday night, Palace aides were quick to correct it," the newspaper crowed. "Now, nowhere on the page is Harry called HRH."

Phew! Sure, the Queen might still be marked as alive, but at least no one's going to make the mistake of calling Prince Harry HRH!

Buckingham Palace explained their poor showing this way: "The Royal Family website contains over five thousand pages of information about the life and work of the Royal Family. Following the death of Her late Majesty Queen Elizabeth II, content has been revisited and updated periodically. Some content may be out of date until this process is complete."

Harry and Meghan didn't read the coverage.

They didn't need to—they already agreed directly with Queen Elizabeth II and her aides years before they'd no longer use their HRH titles.

But no matter. The *Express* newspaper got the clicks and attention they sought, and the major media organizations who followed up on that story did, too.

Chapter 2

Summer's End

Time was passing quickly, and Meghan had now lived as a duchess in her home country nearly as long as she'd lived in England. Harry, who was quite worldly before he met his American wife, was embracing the oddities and differences of life as an expatriate in a unique kind of country.

As Americans know but expatriates can't fully grasp until they get here, the United States is not one amorphous, homogenous land. It is a spectrum of landscapes and personalities and cuisines and attitudes and histories. It is a gameshow where you choose a personality out of fifty states and countless cities. Are you a fit with Arkansas or Manhattan or Oregon? Seattle or Minneapolis or Oklahoma? City to city, state to state, our country will present *very* different opportunities and challenges for those looking to start a new life here.

I've lived in Southern California, and the landscape, both geographically and culturally, is like a different country to my native New England. Mountains, ocean, earthquakes, tsunamis, winds, wildfires, celebrities, droughts, mountain lions, surfing, Malibu, Skid Row, palm trees, Palm Springs and the San Andreas fault.

If you're a prince, you will be welcomed and embraced by celebrities and Hollywood powerbrokers, and Harry slid into the celebrity scene like riding the perfect wave. It made sense, considering he already had friends in California even before meeting Meghan—he'd even experienced that uniquely L.A. phenomenon of waking up in a home only to find its owner is a world-famous celebrity.

In Harry's case, it was 2016, and he and a mate showed up at *Friends* star Courteney Cox's house and, drunk on tequila, Harry bothered Will Arnett and partied with the stars.

In his mega-selling 2023 memoir *Spare*, Harry wrote of Cox, "She was a friend of [my mate's] girlfriend, and had more room. Also, she was traveling, on a job, and didn't mind if we crashed at her place. No complaints from me. As a *Friends* fanatic, the idea of crashing at Monica's was highly appealing. And amusing. But then…Courteney turned up. I was very confused. Was her job canceled? I didn't think it was my place to ask. More: *Does this mean we have to leave?*"

"She smiled. *Of course not, Harry. Plenty of room,*" he recalled. "Great. But I was still confused because… she was Monica. And I was a Chandler. I wondered if I'd ever work up the courage to tell her. Was there enough tequila in California to get me that brave?"

Not long after Harry told us that story, Cox shared her memories of that time.

As the *Friends* legend summed it up, she sort of remembers that English prince, but details are hazy. And his claims there were magic mushrooms on offer had nothing to do with her.

"He did stay here for a couple of days — probably two or three. He's a really nice person," Cox would later tell *Variety*. More recently, Cox said she saw Prince Harry at a birthday party but the pair didn't come face-to-face or get a chance to say hello at the soiree.

I met Courtney at a party when she was still married to David Arquette. They were both lovely, and Courtney was approachable. Sadly, I never got the invite to the Malibu pad, but I did write about it in an interior design magazine, and I can tell you it's an utterly stunning oasis. I can see why Harry remembers that time so fondly.

Harry fit right in as a Californian, and Meghan, as an LA native, was thrilled to have a fully engaged partner in building a new life. By the summer of 2023, the Sussexes were fully ingrained in American life.

If only the British were ready to let them go.

Doesn't it always seem September is a monumental month for the Sussexes? This year would be no different.

Harry was kicking off September by saying goodbye to August. His busiest season began on the twenty-ninth.

As summer puffed its way to its inevitable end, Prince Harry left Meghan and the kids in Montecito and made the 200-mile trip down to San Diego.

It was time to see about some United States military servicemembers and veterans. He'd be doing this one without Meghan, and savvy Sussex watchers had noticed the couple had begun to engage in more and more separate work projects and functions, an event that some viewed as a harbinger of things to come. After all, most couples don't work together all the time, and Harry and Meghan have common ideals but separate talents and interests.

This trip, Harry would make a splash with one thing he cannot be faulted for: his dedication to being there for members of the military around the world.

He walks the walk. He doesn't talk about how much he cares; he turns up. He raises money. He shines a light on the spectrum of life-changing events military families and veterans experience, from heroics to devastating injury to the ultimate sacrifice of giving one's life for one's country.

The AMC Chula Vista theater in San Diego County, California, was buzzing with a carefully selected group of lucky viewers who'd been invited to a special screening of Prince Harry's widely anticipated new Netflix series.

They picked up their popcorn and oversized sodas and streamed into the theater, settling in their comfy seats.

When GraceAnn Skidmore, an author, military spouse and USO volunteer, walked into the theater with her friend Bonnie Pham, she noticed unusually heavy security. Unsure what to make of it, she shrugged and took her seat, ready to get a sneak peek of Netflix's new docuseries *Heart of Invictus*. As Prince Harry himself put it, the show is "the incredible story of competitors brought together through service who are now united through sport."

It is a project near and dear to Harry, who created the Invictus Games Foundation after returning from deployment in Afghanistan and seeing the casualties of war up close. Invictus offers a recovery pathway for international wounded, injured and sick servicemen and women and, as their website explains, "we collaborate to provide opportunities for post-traumatic growth: enabling those involved to reclaim their purpose, identity and future, beyond injury."

Everyone in the Chula Vista theater that night was somehow connected to the military and included servicemembers and their families, veterans, and USO volunteers, as the event was hosted by the USO—a non-profit whose mission is to strengthen America's military service members by keeping them connected to family, home and country.

Skidmore and Pham waited as a hush fell over the room as the presenter took the stage in front of the big screen. It was time to make introductions.

And introduce, they did.

As a hushed audience sat agape, out came the executive producer of that night's entertainment.

Prince Harry grabbed the mic.

"Captain Wales," as he's known fondly by his fellow warfighters, waved and smiled as cheers erupted in the theatre. Skidmore and Pham could hardly believe what they were seeing.

Harry, sunburned, glowing and confident as ever in a cream blazer and white shirt, joked with the crowd he felt at home with. *Always.*

"Nice to see you all," he grinned. "It's nice of you to dress up for the occasion. [No] Suits and ties?"

He turned serious. "I wanted to say a huge thank you for coming out tonight. You guys get to see *Heart of Invictus*, which has been the last two years in the making, sooner than anybody else. It will be coming out on Wednesday, [but] you guys get to watch it tonight. Well, at least two episodes, to sort of whet the appetite for the rest of it."

Pham and Skidmore had their phones out.

A Reel posted on Instagram by @bonnie_pham showed what was going on inside the theater, and viewers could hear Harry talking about the sacrifices service personnel and their families make while serving in the military. The caption: *When it's a random Monday night and Prince Harry crashes the premiere of his show in random Chula Vista.*

Pham added in a comment, *What a show, what a man, what a special surprise! #heartofinvictus.*

For Skidmore, who had only recently volunteered at an adaptive sports event called the Marine Corps trials at Camp Pendleton, Harry's project and his surprise appearance both packed a wallop.

"It was an incredible experience to take my memories of the Marine Corps trials, and couple that with the strength, courage and drive shown in Prince Harry's documentary series," she would later tell San Diego's local NBC news station.

The five-part series, put out by Archewell's production arm, premiered on August 30.

As always, certain media outlets descended like vultures, calling it a "flop" because it failed to make Netflix's top 10 most-streamed programs.

They said this even as the docuseries charmed critics and nailed an 80% fresh rating on Rotten Tomatoes. Harry, the show's participants, and Invictus all received accolades and plenty of good reviews alongside a few sour grapes.

Chapter 3

When September Comes

What better way to kick off an epically busy work month, Meghan thought, than hanging at a Beyoncé concert? Not just any Beyoncé concert, mind you. This was one of the final stops on her *Renaissance* World Tour, and to mark the occasion, the artist asked everyone to turn up in silver. Glittery, celebratory, shining silver.

Meghan and Harry scored coveted tickets thanks to their acquaintanceship with Queen Bey, one that started in London during a star-studded screening of *The Lion King* in 2019. Beyoncé, who voiced Nala, attended the royalty-tinged event along with her husband Jay-Z. Meghan and Beyoncé hit it off immediately, embracing each other and launching into a conversation, with Bey congratulating the duchess on the birth of Archie.

"The baby, so beautiful," Bey gushed. "We love you guys."

Now, in California in 2023, Meghan scanned her wardrobe for just the right piece to assuage Beyoncé's metallic cravings. Clearly, the entertainer had strong feelings about her audience joining in:

"Virgo season is upon us," Bey wrote in an Instagram Stories post in late August. "This tour has been such a joy and as we approach the last month, my birthday wish is to celebrate with you wearing your most fabulous silver fashions to the shows 8.23-9.22! We'll surround ourselves in a shimmering human disco ball each night. Everybody mirroring each other's joy/ Virgo season together in a house of chrome. See you there!"

Meghan had her heart set on something glamorous that could still complement a casual, cool, concert-going look, and eventually settled on silver sequin pencil skirt and a white sleeveless top.

Harry had a tougher time perusing his closet. Having nothing glittery in his wardrobe, he went for a look that *kind of, sort of* complied with Beyoncé's request: He selected a gray shirt and blazer, which he paired with white pants. As one generous *Glamour* magazine writer spun it, "Gray is just the less sparkly version of silver, right?"

Right!

Harry and Meghan met her mum, Doria Ragland, and longtime friend Abigail Spencer, who gets props for turning up looking like a literal disco ball, at the concert and proceeded to settle into a VIP box to enjoy the performance.

They whooped and waved their arms and danced in place and sang along to the spectacular show.

To those who attended the concert and saw the group dancing up in the box, it looked like a blast.

Which meant that *of course* there would be critics coming out of the woodwork in the following days (*insert exhausted sigh*). I mean, going to a concert couldn't just be…going to a concert. Not where Meghan and Harry were concerned.

The headlines in subsequent days slammed Harry and made not-so-subtle jabs at how "miserable," "bored" and "sulky" he was during the show.

His crime? Taking a moment to check his phone and just…breathe. Oh, and he put his hands in his pockets, how dare he. Oh, and looking solemn along with everyone else during a particularly moving moment during Beyoncé's show.

I feel sorry for those people who thought Harry was "miserable," because they've clearly never had the privilege of attending a live show. I wonder if we could start a GoFundMe for them, so they get to experience an hours-long immersive music experience? Who's going to tell them that at some point during any musical concert, you take a moment to yourself? You're tired of gyrating. A particular song doesn't get your blood flowing. It's late. For us over-40s, a concert is all too often held after our bedtime.

In some pictures and videos, Harry was serious and still. In others, he was grinning along with the rest of his friends and family.

It was such a great night, in fact, that Meghan went to see another one.

But first, it was Harry's turn for a boys' night out while Meghan stayed home to spend time with Archie and Lili. On a warm September evening, the Duke of Sussex put on a black suit and shirt and settled into a box at the BMO Stadium in L.A. to enjoy a night of football—aka American soccer—with fan favorite Lionel Messi playing for Inter Miami.

For the prince, the experience felt a bit like being back home, and he smiled and joked with fellow sports fans as Miami won 3-1 against Los Angeles FC.

Major League Soccer's official social media accounts highlighted the royal's attendance, showing Harry chatting with other soccer fans before the game, as well as some of the stars in attendance, including Will Ferrell. (Also in the stands: Leonardo DiCaprio and Selena Gomez; the latter went viral for her wild reaction to LAFC goalkeeper John McCarthy blocking a goal attempt by Messi).

Refreshed and rejuvenated, Harry took over the parenting that same week to make room for Meghan to embark on a girls' night out. Back to Beyoncé she went. The duchess let loose in another silvery outfit alongside Kerry

Washington and Kelly Rowland at SoFi Stadium in Inglewood, California.

Meghan grinned and danced as she took in Beyoncé's birthday celebration show from a box seat, and a lovely photo with her, Washington and Rowland made the rounds the next day.

One thing that did come out of the coverage of that birthday concert: There is some concern for royals reporter-or-commentator Tom Sykes, who I'm not sure was doing too well. He wrote that he sees hidden messages in Meghan's appearance at the concert.

Uh, Tom…Tom?

Under the headline "Meghan Markle Hits Beyoncé Gig, Twice, and Sends a Carefully Curated Message to the Royals," Sykes fills space and yearns for clicks with this hypothesis written in *The Daily Beast*: "It seems Meghan is intent on sending a message with her latest, show-stopping appearance, and it may not be one the Royal Family, this week of all weeks, wish to hear. But she is saying it loud and clear, nonetheless: I'm back."

He fails to explain where she went in order to be able to announce she was back via secret messages no one else heard except Tom. How can you be "back" if you didn't leave?

Raise your hand if you think Meghan, the Duchess of Sussex, is sending coded messages to England via a Beyoncé concert. I'll wait.

Tom, help is available…

Work beckons

The Sussex children and their parents had fallen into a rhythm that everyone was used to by now. Mummy and Papa were all in when they were home, but sometimes, work called them away. Once again, it was time to bid each other farewell.

But ah, there would be a few days' reprieve of sorts, the children learned. Both Harry and Meghan would be traveling to Germany for the Invictus Games, but their attendance would be scattered. Archie and Lilibet said goodbye to their dad from within the cozy walls of their Montecito mansion.

Papa's leaving. Say bye bye, farewell, see you soon!

The children gave kisses, hugs, and they swapped promises to Facetime every day.

Harry flew out first, with Meghan staying back a few extra days to settle the children into their fall routine. Schools in Santa Barbara County start in late August, so they'd only just left their lazy summer days behind and were going back to school along with most of America's children.

Harry was tense as he left home for a multi-leg trip to Europe and the UK. There was a lot riding on the 2023 games, but more stressful was the thought of going home. The UK hadn't been any kind of safe harbour for a while now, considering it was a place where his own father, King Charles III—who early in his reign earned the derogatory nickname King Charles the Cruel in part for the way he's treated Harry—fought tooth and nail to keep his son from receiving much-needed security.

When I tell you that you would not believe some of the threats Harry and his nuclear family receive, I mean you would not believe it. They're specific, cruel, and terrifying. Yet Charles petulantly plays roulette with Harry's safety. For those new to my books, here's the issue: Harry can pay for the most expensive and elite personal security on earth, and in fact does, out of his own pocket. Problem is, these elite teams still won't be a) armed or b) informed and briefed about specific threats toward the prince while in the United Kingdom. For example, if UK law enforcement is in possession of credible information that says an ambush is waiting for Prince Harry around Leicester Square, his private team wouldn't have a clue, and could ostensibly drive him right into it. This puts Harry, Meghan, Archie and Lilibet in immense danger. (Someone get Charles a father-of-the-year mug).

Anyway, in early September Harry slipped into England in time for his beloved WellChild Awards, an event put on by one of the patronages he kept on after leaving his role as an official working royal.

And oh, how this event brought up memories! As Harry donned a freshly pressed white button-down shirt and navy suit, and as he knotted his light blue patterned tie, he was transported back to one year ago when life changed forever.

He and Meghan were preparing to attend these same awards when they received urgent news: doctors, and the royal family, were "concerned" about his grandmother's health. It was obvious what that meant; Queen Elizabeth II's health had been deteriorating for some time, and she was, after all, in her late nineties.

Harry can never forget the moment everything changed.

...a call came in around lunchtime.

Unknown number.

Hello?

It was Pa. Granny's health had taken a turn. She was up in Balmoral, of course. Those beautiful, melancholy late-summer days.

The first thing Harry did was text his brother, William, to ask when he and Kate would be heading up to Scotland to see granny, and by the way—*how* would they be traveling?

Time was of the essence, and the mode of transport mattered. Harry waited impatiently, desperately, for vital information from Prince William, watching the text box on his phone, wanting and needing to see those three dots come up to show his brother was responding.

In times of family crisis, feuds are set aside, bitterness is put on delay, and the bonds of brotherhood are intact underneath it all.

Aren't they?

No reply came.

The Duke and Duchess of Sussex canceled their appearance at WellChild that year, and Harry was left to charter a plane to rush to Scotland to be by his grandma's side at her beloved Balmoral Castle.

Tonight would be different. New year, new life.

Harry showed up to the packed event, whose purpose is always to celebrate the inspirational qualities of the UK's seriously ill children and the professionals who help care for them, in great spirits, putting on his A-game for the little ones (not that it was an effort; he was always charmed within an inch of his life when he met the young ones and their families).

He grinned happily for photos on the red carpet and spent time "with each winner and their families at a pre-ceremony reception, listening to their stories and helping create lifelong memories," sources who were there that night recall.

Later, when the evening was well underway, Harry presented the Award for Inspirational Child (aged 4 to 6). He also felt compelled to share some personal thoughts and feelings about this one-year anniversary, and gave a speech that acknowledged the sadness and shock of the previous September.

"As you know, I was unable to attend the awards last year as my grandmother passed away," the prince told the crowd. "As you also probably know, she would have been the first person to insist I still come to be with you all instead of going to her, and that's precisely why I know, exactly one year on, she is looking down on all of us tonight, happy we are together, continuing to spotlight such an incredible community."

Chapter 4

Daddy Dearest

Prince Harry checked in with his family in California the morning after the awards. Meghan was supportive and shared her husband's bittersweet feelings about the WellChild experience, because she, too, suffered a loss the previous year when her grandmother-in-law died.

Meghan also wished him well for his next emotional wallop, which would involve a dash up the motorway to Windsor Castle. This was a double whammy for Harry, as any Sussex follower understands.

He'd be back in the belly of the beast, going into a family-owned historic castle where he knew some wouldn't welcome him home with open arms.

Then again, he knew his closest family members—father King Charles and elder brother Prince William—would not be at Windsor. Those "close" family members were the ones with which Harry had the most fraught relationship, with William being outright estranged, while Charles seemed to hold open the door a crack.

Or was he? King Charles did not make time to see his youngest son, who was in town from 5,000 miles away, on that visit.

Nope.

They hadn't seen each other in months, but the king simply could not make space in his diary, his aides let it be known via a UK tabloid article.

We know Harry and Charles did not have any contact on that visit. But afterward, when the prince was safely ensconced back in America, King Charles III would let it be known through leaks to the newspapers that he offered Harry a bed at Balmoral—the estate where the queen had died a year before—on September 7, the night of the Well-Child Awards. Charles knew Harry was then heading for Dusseldorf, German, the following day.

Now, I'm not going to project my own opinion about the king's move onto Harry, so I'll simply ask you: Does that offer of a bed in distant Scotland on the same night Harry has a high-profile nighttime engagement in London sound like a father who genuinely wants to see his son? Or does it sound like a passive-aggressive power move that allows him to seem magnanimous and fatherly?

Further, does it seem manipulative to leak this information after the fact, after headlines say you snubbed your son, to make yourself look better? I know what I think. Let me know how you feel online at my Substack, Courtney Hargrove's *Everything is a Mystery.*

It's clear that without Queen Elizabeth's deft handling of family drama and her gravitas from the throne, it's going to be a tough road to reconciliation for Harry, William and Charles, if it ever does happen.

In that week's *People* magazine cover story, their royals reporter wrote of how things had changed in the family as of the first anniversary of the queen's death. "As the late monarch often brought her family together, Prince Harry's rift with the royals seems wider than ever," the reporter wrote. "Fissures within the family came to the fore when King Charles' younger son and his wife, the U.K. for the U.S. in 2020, and relations have remained strained since."

He went on to quote a source close to the royal household.

"I'm sure [the King] misses him," the source said. "Harry is entertaining, warm and very loving as well. And they had a great relationship."

Did they, though? Harry seems to tell a different story. Not long before his current London visit, he'd called out the royals for their lack of "support" after his mother, Princess Diana, died in 1997. In Harry's Netflix documentary "The Heart of Invictus," the prince revealed:

"I didn't have that support structure, that network, or that expert advice to identify what was actually going on with me." And in his memoir, *Spare*, Harry revealed Charles couldn't manage even a simple, single hug when he broke the news to his youngest son that Mummy had been killed and wasn't coming back.

And so it was that Harry made the trip alone to St. George's Chapel at Windsor Castle on September 8, the first anniversary of the queen's death. He dressed in a button-down shirt and slacks, but when he arrived, he was among friends. His cousins Princess Beatrice and Princess Eugenie were there to pay their respects, too. (Regular readers will remember my one encounter with them while dancing in the VIP tent at Cartier Polo at Windsor, slipping on a puddle of beer in my towering wedges, and falling on my ass. I looked up to see two slim, pale hands reaching down for me. "Are you OK?" Beatrice asked, squinting. "I'm good," I replied. I took their hands and regained my composure. Aaaaand stopped dancing immediately. Harry had dashed out of the party by then, so my work was done).

Meanwhile, on that nostalgia-tinged day in September, Charles and Camilla, Harry's stepmother, attended a special church service near Balmoral Castle where the queen died. The king would say in a statement to his subjects:

"In marking the first anniversary of Her late Majesty's death and my Accession, we recall with great affection her long life, devoted service and all she meant to so many of us. I am deeply grateful, too, for the love and support that has been shown to my wife and myself during this year as we do our utmost to be of service to you all."

To mark the occasion, a never-before-seen photograph of Queen Elizabeth II was released. It was taken at Buckingham Palace on Oct. 16, 1968 by Cecil Beaton and selected personally by Charles, according to the palace.

The splintered family was all over the place on that important day. While Harry was at Windsor and Charles was at Balmoral, William and Kate, the Prince and Princess of Wales, remembered the queen during a visit to Wales. They popped in for a private service at St. Davids Cathedral, and they shared photos of the queen on their social media channels.

They didn't find a moment to visit with Harry. And don't say they're too busy. Billionaires Kate and William work a few full days a year. As Graham Smith of the abolish-the-monarchy group Republic explained, in 2023, "Although spun as showing a hard-working family, the numbers suggest the royals do the equivalent of no more than two months of full-time work each year.

"William has carried out just 172 engagements, which amounts to less than one month full-time equivalent work. Kate did even less, with just 123 engagements. **Engagements last an average of one hour, although many are much shorter.**

"It takes a deep sense of entitlement and a complete lack of serious scrutiny for William, Kate and the others to rake in multi-million pound fortunes, to enjoy the status and privileges of their positions while doing so little," Smith added in his analysis.

Back home in Santa Barbara, Meghan was working on projects the public knew nothing about.

And you know a duchess gotta eat, right?

One lunchtime she was craving the double-double you can only get at In-N-Out Burger, one of the Sussex's guilty pleasures.

Meghan and a member of her staff rolled up to the fast-food drive-thru in Goleta, an enclave not far from Santa Barbara Airport and a 15-minute drive from the Sussex manse in Montecito.

Meghan's always camera-ready at the drive-thru because she knows the employees will do a double-take when they see her and/or Harry, and will often take a photo—and she has fun with it. As she rolled up in a black Range Rover on a lazy Sunday afternoon in a luxury model valued at six figures, the duchess was casual-cool, sporting a slicked-back ponytail and black shades.

She ordered with a smile, and the staff were already beginning to chatter about the famous royal visitor at the restaurant.

Without Harry's usual hefty order, the day would be a bargain. The staff knows the Sussex family's preferences, but this time the prince wasn't there to order—wait for it—TWO double-doubles animal style (this is a secret menu involving lots of mustard), fries, and a Coke.

Prince Harry and apparently the employees at the burger chain know Meghan's order by heart, too, he once said.

"In-N-Out is the best!" Harry says. "I order two double-doubles, animal style, fries and a Coke. And that's just for me. Meg gets the cheeseburger and fries with sides of jalapeños. I just stick with ketchup and that special sauce of theirs. So good!"

This time, Meghan got milkshakes to go, too, and off she and her companion, a young woman, went to deliver the food back to their house.

Naturally, the milkshakes, those sweet, frothy summer drinks, would cause an international kerfuffle.

If you've been following this series at all, you've already guessed that, right?

A milkshake, when sipped by the Duchess of Sussex, is never just a milkshake.

That Invictus spirit

Meghan, Harry and the Archewell team had prepared within an inch of their lives for both royals to travel to Germany in September of 2023 for the Invictus Games.

They knew the turf well, having traveled there in 2022 for the Invictus Games Düsseldorf 2023 One Year to Go event. Back then, the crowds went bananas when Meghan and Harry walked a red carpet hand-in-hand. They greeted their fans and again, the images created for posterity that day are in stark contrast to pervasive, made-up claims that the couple is not popular. Wherever they go, they are mobbed with fans who adore them, as evidenced by videos taken at every event at One Year to Go.

Now it was time for the games, and Harry arrived in the German city of Dusseldorf on Friday, September 9, like a gale-force wind. The Duke of Sussex was immediately met and embraced by the mayor, German Defense Minister Boris Pistorius, and a pack of cheering fans. But the prince didn't have time for a crowd visit; he was whisked into City Hall for a reception.

The Invictus Games were held at Duesseldorf's Merkus Spiel arena, as was the opening ceremony. Harry took the stage and gave an emotional and humorous speech to kick things off.

He paid tribute to the athletes competing in the days-long games, all of them wounded, injured or sick military personnel or veterans.

He was excited to announce some new nations that had joined the Invictus Games since their last event in 2022: Colombia, Israel and Nigeria were now part of the Invictus family.

Harry paused and surveyed his rapt audience.

"Now," he added, "I'm not saying we play favourites in our home, but since my wife has discovered she is of Nigerian descent, it's likely to get a little more competitive this year."

That drew some chuckles, and the tone of the evening, and the days ahead, was set.

While Harry was watching some of the competitions for a few days, Meghan woke up that Monday morning and said goodbye to her two little scamps. Then she took off for Germany. Upon landing, she was whisked to the five-star Hyatt Regency where she and Harry would reside in the presidential suite. She settled in, freshened up, and changed.

The duchess went straight out to the Family & Friends party with Prince Harry.

Bright-eyed and beaming, the duchess told the crowd, "It is so special to be here. I'm so sorry that I was a little late for the party."

She gave a shout-out to Fischer House, a foundation that provides a home away from home for military and veteran families while their loved ones are hospitalized.

"Just like so many of you, we know this is about family and friends and the community that Invictus has created, that Fischer House has created, and so I had to just spend a little bit more time getting our little ones settled home," Meghan said. "Getting milkshakes, doing school drop off, and then I just landed a couple of hours ago. I am thrilled that the first event that I can do with Invictus is here with all of you."

She concluded her speech with a rousing bit of motivation for the Invictus athletes.

"There are so many people we know back home who are rooting for all of you, even if they can't be here, they are here in spirit. Thank you, thank you also for this amazing band and we're looking forward to such a fantastic week.

"Have the best time, we're cheering for you, and we can't wait to bring our kids also so they can experience just how awesome this is," she concluded. "Thank you guys so, so much."

Now, go back and read that again if you have to.

Can you spot the scandal in Meghan's speech?

So, *so* much scandal.

Just listen to Angela Levin, who writes about and talks about the royals a lot.

After Meghan's speech, Angela called the duchess "patronizing" during an appearance on Sky News Australia. "You know, she's saying she's so sorry she's late. But she had to get some milkshakes for her children and take the older one to school; it's so patronizing. To assume that everybody is so stupid that they know she could be three days late because she wanted to take the older child to school is nonsense. We're not that stupid, thank you."

Angela wasn't done, though.

"Don't think for a second she doesn't have a lot of help there [at the couple's Montecito, CA home]," Levin mopes. "[Meghan's] not the sort of woman, and I don't blame her for this, who wants to look after children all day long. She wants to promote herself."

Now, I generally don't repeat bile from bitter trolls here (no, really. For every snotty, bullying line you see in this series, there are a million I ignore). Don't feed them; don't give them oxygen. Sometimes, though, they're a part of Sussex history, because the vitriol spreads like a virus, grows like weeds, infects and invades comment sections, social media, and then, again, the mainstream media. Levin's pointless milkshake hate did just that, and it left Meghan wondering what she could possibly to do get them to leave her the hell alone. Also, this one was just ultra weird. Picking on a mother for staying home…and then *not* staying home…it was both weird and nonsensical.

And yet this kind of unprompted criticism continues to this day.

Meat and potatoes and beer, oh my!

When you're a world-traveling prince, you never know where you'll be when your birthday hits.

For Harry, 39 would be celebrated in Dusseldorf.

The night before his September 15 birthday, the Sussexes and their traveling team of Archewell and Invictus colleagues found a cheerful restaurant, an ultra-German, meat-heavy, foamy beer-stein filled place called Im Goldenen Kessel.

The royal couple went casual, befitting the week's sporty theme. Meghan donned nude ballet flats and white skinny jeans, and Harry chose blue jeans and a grey shirt.

Their party took up two tables in the main dining area and thankfully, staff were on the spot to help them order, as all their menus are in German only. Meghan and Harry cuddled and laughed together in the cozy restaurant, as tactile away from the cameras as they are when the world is watching.

They went full local, leaning into the stodge factor (for those who don't know Brit-speak, "stodge" is filling, starchy, and/or heavy food that fills you up), ordering Wiener Schnitzel, pork knuckle, bratwurst, and plates of roasted and mashed potatoes.

Harry's theme of the night was YOLO, apparently. The fit prince washed the artery-cloggers he'd ordered down with six beers. Meghan sipped one small beer.

Their friends and colleagues toasted the prince, and the restaurant brought out a white-chocolate cake, serenading him as other restaurant patrons looked on. Not long before midnight and the onset of Harry's actual birthday, the prince picked up the tab. And even though Europe has a relaxed tipping policy, mostly because their staff are paid fair wages, Harry tipped handsomely for the staff's wonderful treatment of him and his friends. (This European way is in comparison the United States where restaurants are required to pay literal pennies and where servers wages are $2.13 per hour. Yes, non-Americans, you read that right. Next time you visit and sneer at the tipping culture and decide to stiff your server, remember that number. Most tourists are lovely and understand the cultural differences. But I've met too many jerks in my travels not to make this point).

Harry, Meghan and the group left the restaurant just before midnight and walked along the cobblestoned streets of Old Town alongside their security team and a police escort, one provided by local government, the kind that the Sussexes are not even given in Harry's home country.

The prince woke up the next morning a bit worse for wear, but was buoyed once again by the spirit of Invictus. The day's celebration of his pre-milestone 39th birthday began when he was serenaded by the crowd at the sitting volleyball game between Poland and Germany with a personalized version of "Happy Birthday."

While complete strangers took time out of their day to wish Harry well in a very public way, it was crickets from his family back in England. Why did none of them toss him a happy birthday on social media, you ask? Who really knows. The official line is that after Charles took the throne and became King Charles III, his courtiers mumbled something about how only working royals would heretofore get birthday shout-outs on their social media accounts, including on Buckingham Palace's (Charles and Camilla) and Kensington Palace's (William and Kate).

So Charles's second son's birthday went unmarked by his fellow royals, the people who are allegedly supposed to love and support him the most.

Chapter 5

Denial Ain't Just a River in Egypt

There is a group of men, all of them in their sixties, who spent years employed by London's Metropolitan Police force, known as the Met. These six fine fellows all held positions with the elite Parliamentary and Diplomatic Protection branch, which guards politicians and diplomats.

Thanks to technology like WhatsApp, the guys—Michael Chadwell, Peter Booth, Trevor Lewton, Anthony Elsom, Alan Hall and Robert Lewis—were able to keep in touch after retiring from the force. They created a lively messaging group with the folksy, grandpa-friendly label "Old Boys Beer Meet—Wales."

The guys engaged in an ongoing chat where they could share jokes, life updates, observations, and, as it turned out, offensive bouts of racism. Apart from the presumed "Where do you want to meet for a pint?" type of messages, these men sprinkled in racist "jokes" and observations. Three of the messages included racist comments about Meghan and Harry. One of them, sent by Trevor Lewton in

March 2022, included a photo of an aspirin bottle. The caption?

Why do they put cotton wool in tablet bottles? To remind Black people they were cotton pickers before they were drug dealers.

The former Met officers, who had held positions of power over many vulnerable UK subjects and people of color during their careers, didn't stop there. They got their jollies sharing racist comments about the UK government's Rwanda policy, deadly floods in Pakistan, and Rishi Sunak, Britain's first prime minister of color.

And then they got caught.

The men's offensive chit-chat was found out *not* by their former colleagues—crack investigators with state-of-the-art equipment and resources—but by the media. A BBC Newsnight investigation uncovered the retired officers' messages, which had been sent between August 2018 and September 2022. A police investigation followed, with the force reacting when their hand was forced by media reports, rather than being proactive in eradicating racism and hate in their ranks.

In 2023, five of the retired officers pleaded guilty at London's Westminster Magistrates' Court to sending by public communication grossly offensive racist messages. Chadwell was the only man to contest his one charge; he lost. All six beer-drinking buffoons were eventually given suspended prison sentences of up to 14 weeks each.

Lewton, who had been diagnosed with lung cancer, later contested his sentence, and his case would later be heard in December of 2024 (I'm making a rare foray into the future to close this story out here and now). He was asked what he wanted to achieve with the appeal. Lewton replied in part, "I think a suspended sentence for one joke made when I was gravely vulnerable, I could have sent inadvertently, is excessive."

Judge Justin Cole read out loud in court the message that whiny Lewton had sent, and then the disgusted judge revealed his reaction to the gallery.

"To any reasonable person," Judge Cole said, "this is grossly offensive racism. It's not in any way in context. It's simply repellent racism in its rawest form."

Next came my favorite part, because it reveals the judge's relatable frustration at the impossible task of trying to educate every "well-meaning" person who wants to be free to say racist things while maintaining they're not racist. Said the judge that December,

"You still describe it as a joke. You still make reference to comedians using this type of material. We are not sure you really get it."

And so the case was closed.

What does this have to do with Harry and Meghan? Apart from anything else, this crackdown, these consequences, send the vital message that Harry and Meghan's years of sounding the alarm about the racism she's faced in Britain across all classes and power structures is not paranoia or "wokeness" (god forbid).

It is real, and it is writ large in this case. Or, should I say, writ small, writ stupid, and writ indiscreetly on a multi-member WhatsApp group.

Meghan and Harry packed their things for that most exhausting of travel considerations: the multi-season trip. They'd be hitting New York in the autumnal chill of October, taking part in a panel for a summit for World Mental Health Day.

But, after that, they'd also be gifting themselves time in the sun to reconnect, recharge, and take a break from the hamster wheel of preparing for and attending events for which they always had to be camera-ready.

H, don't forget the swim trunks I bought you. The new ones.

M, do you have the sunscreen?

Check. I'll be wearing white for the panel. Which suits are you bringing?

Meghan and Harry left Prince Archie and Princess Lilibet in safe hands in Montecito and headed to the airport to catch their flight to New York. As always, they worked on the plane, talking through the logistics and the message they wanted to put out at this vital event.

This one was special. On Tuesday, Oct. 10, the Sussexes would be putting on the Archewell Foundation's first-ever face-to-face, live event. This one was personal, too, as they'd invited parents who'd been through the ringer and suffered terrible losses related to their children's social media use. Both Meghan and Harry were prepared to offer rare comments about parenting their own children, as they felt it was the least they could do in a room full of grieving, traumatized and/or emotional parents who'd suffered terribly from social media abuse and cruelty.

The duke and duchess, on a New York City stage, spoke of fears, and of hope, for the future when their little ones, Prince Archie and Princess Lilibet, would be old enough to dive into social media and face the spectrum of both connection and damage.

"As parents, though our kids are really young, 2 1/2 and 4 1/2, but social media isn't going away," Meghan told the audience. "And by design, there was an entry post that was supposed to be positive and create community, but something has devolved."

Harry added, "I think for us, for myself and my wife, with kids growing up in a digital age, the priority here is to again turn pain into purpose and provide as much support as well as a spotlight and a platform for these parents to come together, to heal, to grieve."

It was a successful one-week trip to the city that never sleeps, albeit one that spawned more critical headlines out of Britain, but we won't be giving that side of it any oxygen.

And then it was off to paradise.

Harry and Meghan surveyed their beachy, airy suite and flopped out on the all-white canopy bed. Just a quick second to be still, that was all. The traveling and the working and the parenting and…

They both exhaled. Markus had done it again. Meghan was already planning for a thank-you note and small gift, whether flowers or gourmet food, to send to her longtime friend Markus Anderson, a hotelier and man-about-town who's famous in the Sussex fandom for his secret-squirrel operation to set the pair up on their first date in 2016. Back then it had been a sultry July night at Dean Street Townhouse, a Soho House location in London.

This week it was Soho Beach House Canouan, a stunning beachfront resort on a lovely private island a hair away from the hurricane belt. This is a place that the famous "they" label as an under-the-radar getaway where "billionaires can escape millionaires." There's a runway for private jets and a marina built for megayachts.

The Sussexes got moving before they were tempted to nap. They were, after all, on a very special island, just a dot on the map of a vast ocean, one of several islands part of St. Vincent and the Grenadines.

That week, Meghan and Harry would dress down and let the hot breeze overcome them, then cool off in the water off the private Grand Bay Beach steps away from their room (they call them "rooms," but they're more like suites, nearly 800 square feet with a separate dining area).

They could throw a coconut and reach the beach bar with its thatched roof set among the palm trees.

They also ventured out of the resort with their security team, checking out the shops and restaurants on the promenade at the Sandy Lane Yacht Club and Marina in Glossy Bay. Meghan, going beach casual in an ivory maxi dress and Panama hat, wanted to check out Faye, a gourmet grocery store that offers an "exclusive selection of fresh seasonal organic products, from vegetables to cheeses, sweets, seafood and exclusive meat cuts" imported from France. They browsed the shelves there, and when they emerged, she and Harry held hands as they headed to the tender that would whisk them back to their side of the three-mile-wide island.

Chapter 6

November

Prince Harry had taken a break from military matters after the September Germany trip, pivoting to his production work and spending time with his family.

But then November hit, and he was back to thinking about his fellow servicemembers and veterans, as the United States would be recognizing Veterans' Day that month.

Both Harry and Meghan would, as always, find a way to mix business and pleasure. The pair works hard and plays hard, and when they were invited on a private jet with some friends and acquaintances to pop over to Las Vegas for a big concert, they were *in*.

They kissed Prince Archie and Princess Lili goodbye and assured them it would be nothing more than an extended date night, even if it did involve leaving on a jet plane.

Mummy and Papa will be home when you wake up in the morning, they promised.

Harry and Meghan stepped into their black Range Rover and, as their security team buffered them from any threats to be found outside their sprawling retreat, they drove through the cool November breezes floating through Santa Barbara.

Thus commenced one of the Sussexes' most controversial and scrutinized nights out of the year.

The photos that went around the world of the first leg of their journey that day warmed the hearts of some, and stoked the fires of envy in others.

Their security team escorted them across the tarmac at Santa Barbara Airport as distant palm trees bent to the wind's will. Friends were already waiting for them alongside a private Gulfstream—a G4 to be precise—owned by Texas oil heir Michael Herd. The privileged few would be treated to the VIP experience at Katy Perry's final show of her residency in Sin City.

Actor Cameron Diaz grinned as Zoe Saldana pulled Diaz's rocker husband Benji Madden into a big hug. Also aboard the flight from Santa Barbara was legendary movie producer David Katzenberg and billionaire Bumble dating app founder Whitney Wolfe Herd.

These were Harry and Meghan's neighbors now. Celebrities are part and parcel of life in Montecito. Cameron, who'd quit acting to spend more time with daughter Raddix Chloe Wildflower Madden, then age 4, was having some adjustment issues as she returned to the film world. Like many actors who tire of the grind, she pivoted to business, launching the successful wine brand Aveline, and basing herself in Montecito with her family in 2022.

The Duke and Duchess also live near Perry and her longtime love Orlando Bloom, a glamorous couple who purchased an ocean-view compound in Montecito in 2020 from former Duracell and Chrysler CEO C. Robert Kidder.

The group landed in Vegas after the forty-minute flight and went out for dinner before the show. Harry and Meghan, dressed mostly in black, chatted away with others in the VIP box and had a blast at Perry's show. It was all very rock-n-roll, and it was over before they knew it.

The jet touched down in Santa Barbara at one a.m., and, as promised, Meghan and Harry were home to have breakfast with their children.

Which was nice.

But the following day, the British tabloids, whose reporters and editors were apparently sitting around twiddling their thumbs on a slow news day, decided to generate some of their own. In the usual tabloid circle-jerk that makes the rounds as one publication and website puts it down and another picks it up, a tabloid published a story about how Harry and Meghan are "eco-hypocrites" for sharing a private jet for a forty-minute flight! HYPO-CRITES, I tell you!

As always, and as I've addressed here in the past, this is an old trick. Cherry-picking big names for heavy handed accusations and blame is a cudgel used by *actual* climate destroyers as misdirection.

There is, in fact, a common comeback employed by true climate warriors who are used to these kinds of misleading headlines. The response goes something like this: Sure, it's fair to discuss whether Taylor Swift's personal jet is taking up far more than her fair share of carbon emissions and if that makes her and her ilk—like Tom Brady, Leo DiCaprio, Prince William and Princess Kate, who use helicopters for personal travel like we use cars to the grocery store—bad for the environment and setters of a bad example.

But—and this is a big but—the primary carbon-emissions villains are not celebrities sharing jets for quick trips. The villains are large-scale fleets owned by greedy corporations, politicians, and industries known for massive carbon footprints the world over.

These include corporations like the one who owns the tabloid that created the eco-hypocrite "story," Rupert Murdoch and his News Corp. Talk about hypocrisy. We see you, Rupert and sons. Using the relatively small footprint of an individual celebrity and private jet to explain climate change is an old, weak, unhelpful strategy.

Stories about celebrity private jets divert attention away from more critical issues like industrial practices, energy production, and policy changes needed to address climate change at a larger scale.

And so these accusatory headlines about celebrity hypocrisy, in this case Prince Harry and Duchess Meghan, coming from the climate-change-denying, eco-flouting billionaires who own these "news" organizations, are a distraction. They treat their readers like dogs watching squirrels. *I'm a billionaire who's not paying my fair share of taxes, I'm taking private jets everywhere and backing causes that will destroy our earth for future generations, but look over there at the big shiny, pretty celebrity!*

Michael Herd, part owner of the Gulfstream, had a snappy retort to tabloids who contacted him for comment on their non-story. Meghan and Harry, he said, "just went to dinner and to see Katy's last show. They're nice people."

Do you have comment on criticism hurled at the Sussexes? Asked the reporter.

"No. I'm not them," Herd pointed out to the hapless scribe.

I don't know what was said in the Sussex home the day after the Katy Perry concert, but it wouldn't surprise me if it involved some of the tentpoles of the argument I just made.

Thank U, next.

Time to buckle down now. Prince Harry always takes the ceremony and gravity around Veterans Day (in the U.S.) and Remembrance Sunday (UK) very seriously. Harry is a military veteran himself. He served for ten years in the British Army, reaching the rank of captain and seeing battle in a way the other men in his family never did.

"Two tours in Afghanistan, flying Apache helicopters on a military base, means that you grow up pretty fast. Jeez, I went to war twice," Harry reflected in the Sussexes' 2022 Netflix series.

In the run-up to Veterans Day 2023, Harry and Meghan traveled through their home state paying their respects. Before they departed, they read the literature their staff had prepared for them about the military bases, and familiarized themselves with the biographical information about the people they'd be meeting.

Harry also conducted a virtual visit for the 17th Annual Stand Up for Heroes benefit to celebrate America's veterans and their families. Standing proudly in front of the camera wearing the military medals he'd earned, the same ones he'd been banned from wearing at his father's coronation only a few months earlier, the prince started off lightheartedly, joking about his "reiki healer" and being ginger (in America, ginger=redhead), but then he brought it back to the solemn nature of what they were there for.

"I've said it before and I'll say it again, service is what happens in the quiet and the chaos," Harry said. "And whether we are wearing the uniform or not, we must continue to uphold the values we learned side by side on the base, on the drill square and on the battlefield."

Next on the agenda to recognize veterans was a quiet visit to Marine Corps Camp Pendleton in San Diego. Archewell's PR team shared later that day that the royal couple "spent the morning with veteran and active duty service members and their loved ones."

It was a lovely visit, sources say, and when it was completed, the Duke and Duchess of Sussex headed out to take part in the grand opening of the Navy SEAL Foundation's Warrior Fitness Program West Coast facility. Meghan and Harry watched as the foundation CEO Robin King cut the ribbon, and then the pair waved at the crowd as they stepped into the building for a tour of the brand-new facility.

Harry was somber, his body language closed, as the event unfolded. Meghan was more animated, giving Harry space to have a moment of quietude as he took in the importance of the day.

King, for her part, was impressed by the famous pair's deep knowledge of the program and its goals.

"They were absolutely fantastic. They had done a lot of homework on the Navy SEAL Foundation, on the program," she would later tell *People*. "I was thoroughly impressed with both of them on how much they wanted to engage with the community members to talk about the real issues."

For those who think doing your basic homework is a given, and who might wonder why anyone would attend an event unprepared, know that it happens all the time. High-profile people are often too busy or too uninterested to do anything but show up and smile, then go back to what they really want to be doing.

For example, there was once a princess who turned up for a special tour of a fancy food store called Fortnum and Mason. Her Majesty Queen Elizabeth II was there too, charming everyone she came into contact with. It was the queen's Diamond Jubilee year, and she was dragging along two other senior royal women on the trip.

One of the royals checked out a sampling of the store's legendary teas laid out in ramekins that would've been giving off a cornucopia of scents. The princess picked one up and, with a straight face, asked one of the tea experts, "Can you test the smell by smelling it?"

To avoid such embarrassing gaffes, one should do one's homework before attending any event, even one involving nothing more intellectual than tea and pastries.

Harry's family back in England, meanwhile, were seen paying somber respects at the National Service of Remembrance, an annual ceremony held during the second weekend of November.

They joined politicians, service personnel and veterans in London. On a balcony above The Cenotaph war memorial in England's capital, Kate Middleton, the Princess of Wales, stood alongside Queen Camilla. The pair looked on as their husbands, Prince William and King Charles, laid wreaths at the memorial during the service.

No one knew that would be one of the last public sightings of Kate Middleton for a long, long time.

Chapter 7

December is for Slaying Dragons

Christmas came early for Prince Harry. On December 14, the seeds he'd sown from 2019 through June 2023 sprouted like sunflowers in summer.

The ruling came down from his native England on a Friday morning: He'd won his phone hacking lawsuit against Mirror Group Newspapers, and was awarded over £140,000 (around $180,000).

The presiding judge in London's High Court ruled that fifteen of thirty-three published articles at the heart of Harry's complaint against Mirror Group Newspapers "were the product of phone hacking of his mobile phone or the mobile phones of his associates, or the product of other unlawful information-gathering."

This moral victory could not be understated in casa de Sussex that day.

The win came at a personal cost to him; a flight across a continent and an ocean, time away from his wife and children, and eight hours of exhausting cross-examination, all of which could have been avoided if he had decided not to take a stand. If he hadn't insisted on personally calling out the rabid, amoral media in his country.

While the trial was going on, Harry, who had told the court that "every single article has caused me distress" and that tabloids have "blood on their hands," had fielded rigorous, forensic questioning by top legal minds in front of the world's media long before this December 2023 decision.

When his testimony was nearly over, Harry's barrister had noted the toll the hours had taken on the prince, and asked in front of those same kind of journalists who'd got them to this point in the first place, what the experience had been like for him.

Harry took time to answer. After a long pause, the prince said only, "It's a lot."

Some reporters remarked the prince looked close to tears by the time he'd finished, clearly spent, giving everything he had to bring down a twisted system no single person could dismantle alone.

And so on the day of the ruling in wintry December 2023, Harry's lawyer David Sherbourne read the prince's statement outside court. Harry, via his lawyer, called the victory "vindicating and affirming."

"Today is a great day for truth as well as accountability. I've been told that slaying dragons will get you burned. But in light of today's victory and the importance of doing what is needed for a free and honest press, it's a worthwhile price to pay. The mission continues," he said.

Harry wasn't in court for the ruling "due to the short notice which was given of this hearing," his lawyer explained. Instead, Harry made sure to watch via a video feed.

Hours later, the Sussexes released their 2023 holiday card. Obviously, someone was going to have a problem with it, because what is life without being angry for absolutely no reason?

The card was an extremely offensive image (insert sarcasm emoji) from the closing ceremony of the Invictus Games in Dusseldorf back in September. Harry was clad in a black suit with a black dress shirt underneath, and Meghan wore a green strapless dress with delicate laser-cut flower details. The virtual greeting card was sent via email on behalf of their Archewell organization.

"We wish you a very happy holiday season. Thanks for all the support in 2023!" The card read, controversially.

You know a couple is consummate clickbait, big earners for the media, when a bit of negative chatter on social media becomes a headline in a major metropolitan newspaper.

The New York *Post*, another Murdoch special, blared,

'Losers' Meghan Markle and Prince Harry reveal their 2023 holiday card: 'Where the hell are the kids?'

Social media and the tabloids coexist in a circle of hell, so it's hard to tell where one ends and the other begins, but they were all given the same talking points that day.

"No children, no family, no friends," quipped @MeghansMole on social media. "The biggest losers of 2023."

Does this strike anyone as a normal response to a holiday card no one has to click on if they don't want to?

I don't know about Meghan and Harry, but I'll tell you that if there were weirdos out there showing such desperation and entitlement to see my children, I'd call security. The obsession is…well, that's why they have a crack security team.

The good news was, none of that mattered to the happy couple. They'd already taken off with their little ones to peaceful, sunny climes for a holiday break.

Their security team surrounding them as always, Meghan, Harry, Lilibet and Archie boarded a plane for the long journey down to Central America.

Costa Rica, to be specific.

They kept the details of their vacation under wraps and out of the prying eyes of tabloid reporters, a feat they've become adept at, more so than anyone gives them credit for. They stayed in a private home rather than a resort, with unconfirmed reports they were in a sprawling beachfront villa in the gated community of Monte Bello.

Two grainy, long-lens shots caught them, first in a golf cart with Harry and Archie, and another with petite Meghan carrying a tired Lilibet, her strawberry blonde hair in a frayed, beachy ponytail. It was a peaceful pre-Christmas idyll where all four could be together and start some new holiday traditions.

Meghan was asked around that time what her favorite Christmas tradition was. She replied, "We're creating new ones now that our little ones are growing up. And we're enjoying every moment of it…I love trimming and decorating the tree with my children."

There was one thing Meghan and Harry laughingly admitted they *wouldn't* be doing this year, and it involved a certain holiday gift. Prince Archie, at the ripe old age of 4 ½, was showing a talent for photography. It helps, of course, when your close family friend is shutterbug extraordinaire Misan Harriman. Uncle Misan—I made up this moniker, I have no idea if the Sussex kids call him that—is already mentoring the young prince, and was, as Meghan explains, "showing him how to do photography the last time he was with us, and I bought Archie a camera, and he said, 'But it's not a Leica like Misan.'"

The duchess added with a laugh that the iconic (and pricey) camera brand was not suitable for a child not even out of first grade. "I said, 'You are not getting a Leica! Not even for Christmas."

That December was so quiet for the Sussexes that, as the month and the year hurtled toward their end, the media was reduced to putting out a series of dull articles speculating, guessing and lying about what the couple had done or might do in the future.

But five thousand miles away from Montecito, the public life of another senior British royal woman was about to explode in an unholy mess, the likes of which had never been seen before.

PART II:

Duchess Disappeared

Chapter 8

Wintering

Tucked in an old colonial in the frigid, snowy hills of New England, I was huddled over my laptop, space heater humming, putting the finishing touches on a novella about Duchess Scarlett and Prince Alexander.

The idea for a story about a royal couple who looked perfect on the outside but held secrets that could destroy them both came to me two months earlier, and I'd written the mini-novel during the autumn, plotting it carefully and adding the realistic touches I'd absorbed from years covering the royals up close and from afar.

The book, a sequel to my 2022 royal-infused psychological suspense novella *The Silent Duchess*, was given a publication date of December 19, 2023.

Here is the jacket copy my publisher, One Moment Books, posted with the Kindle version of *Duchess Disappeared*:

With Scarlett suddenly out of the public eye after that last dinner with her husband, the world outside Westercoate Manor has begun asking questions on social media, in private conversations among the country's sharp-eyed, intrusive royal reporters, and even some suspicious media outlets outside the country. Everyone's asking the same question: Where is Duchess Scarlett?

Keep this language in the back of your mind as you read what happened within the British royal family in the weeks after that jacket copy was posted on book retailer websites.

Now.

I'm not saying I'm clairvoyant, but I am fascinated by how many eerie, spot-on premonitions have come true with my books.

Take my book *London Bridge is Down* for another example. The nonfiction book, which revealed the historic secret government and royal family plans to handle the many events to take place after Queen Elizabeth II's death, was put up for preorder on book retailer websites on September 3, 2022, having been completed weeks before. The publication date was set for September 10, 2022. The queen died September 8, 2022.

But wait, there's more.

Most recently, the cover of this very book, which you can see is covered in flowers blooming in the stunning colors of pink lemonade and accents of hot pink, and said flowers are growing on a tree branch, was posted February 19, 2025 when my publisher put this book up for preorder on book retailer websites. On February 24, 2025, Meghan posted an Instagram story showing a video she took of beautiful flowers growing on a tree branch in the exact color of this book cover, in that same beautiful pink lemonade with accents of hot pink.

There was something else, too, going on that winter that parallelled Kate Middleton, the Princess of Wales, but it had nothing to do with being psychic and everything to do with coincidence and bad luck in my own life.

#WhereIsKate?

Everything appeared normal to the average outsider. Kate and William, the Princess and Prince of Wales, appeared as expected for the holidays in Norfolk, where they have a sprawling manor known as Anmer Hall, which sits on King Charles's Sandringham Estate.

With them were their three young children, George, Charlotte and Louis. Christmas at the British royal family's Sandringham estate meant the traditional walk to church would be publicly photographed and scrutinized as cheering plebians, corralled behind ropes, lined the path to give the royals gifts and holiday wishes. During that day's stroll, Kate grinned, flashed her dimples, looked radiant in blue, and shook hands as she kept a close eye on her three children.

There were plans for early spring already in the diary. One trip in particular had been scheduled and announced days before: Will and Kate would be heading to Italy. On December 22, the *Daily Mail* had run a story touting their exclusive scoop about the short trip.

No one knew then that would be the last time Kate would be seen in public for a very long time.

Starting just after December 28 and continuing for months to come, social media would be flooded with claims that there had been ambulances making a spectacle around the Sandringham estate in Norfolk that day. This is uncorroborated, as far as I've been able to discern, and unless more evidence is presented, cannot be called anything more than rumor.

But there *was* that dramatic VIP convoy on the same day, captured on video in London, complete with police escort and the royal-favored Range Rovers. Where you find a royal convoy, you'll almost always find a Range Rover.

Curious, indeed. But still nothing to be alarmed about.

January 2024

The new year dawned with the rise of the hopeful yet brutal month of January, loathed by all except perhaps polar bears, and the royals weren't doing anything of note.

Meghan and Hary were in hibernation, forcing a click-hungry media to make up stories based on old news, opinions, and guesses. Examples included out-of-thin-air claims that their relationship is no longer "passionate," and, holy desperate rehashes Batman, "The Royal Drama Over Harry, Meghan and Lilibet's Name is Back." (Spoiler alert: It wasn't back).

British subjects were returning to work with tighter pants and lingering hangovers, grumpily yet valiantly attempting Dry January or optimistically leaping into diets and pricey gym memberships.

The royal family was met with grey skies and blustery winds same as everyone else, and in fact, everything around the royal family seemed to be proceeding as normal. *Seemed* to be, that is, until Kensington Palace, which in this book is synonymous with the offices of Prince William and Princess Kate, told the world things were most decidedly *not* normal.

Bear in mind this was not a time when people were sitting at home thinking to themselves, *Hmm...we haven't seen Kate Middleton, the Princess of Wales, since her walk at Sandringham a couple weeks ago. Wonder what's up with her?*

It's fair to say that had Kensington Palace not offered up a statement at all, as many royal watchers pointed out at the time, no one would've realized there was a problem.

Oh, but there was.

A problem, that is. And it was a big one.

I'm including the full statement as it was posted on January 17 by Kensington Palace (Prince William) on the royal family's official website, Royal.uk, because this was utterly unprecedented.

Never in the history of the royal family has a preemptive statement been issued about a senior royal's very vague health condition. The bombshell news dropped on a normal, run-of-the-mill Wednesday.

It went like this:

No one: *Where is the Princess of Wales?*

Prince William: *My wife, the Princess of Wales, just had surgery and you won't see her for a very long time.*

Wait…*what?*

Read the full statement for yourself:

Her Royal Highness The Princess of Wales was admitted to hospital yesterday for planned abdominal surgery. The surgery was successful and it is expected that she will remain in hospital for ten to fourteen days, before returning home to continue her recovery. Based on the current medical advice, she is unlikely to return to public duties until after Easter.

The Princess of Wales appreciates the interest this statement will generate. She hopes that the public will understand her desire to maintain as much normality for her children as possible; and her wish that her personal medical information remains private.

Kensington Palace will, therefore, only provide updates on Her Royal Highness' progress when there is significant new information to share.

The Princess of Wales wishes to apologise to all those concerned for the fact that she has to postpone her upcoming engagements. She looks forward to reinstating as many as possible, as soon as possible.

The statement was confusing at best, misleading at worst.

For starters, the statement came *after* the surgery, which set things off on rocky footing. Out of nowhere, Prince William's office announced to the world that Kate Middleton, the Princess of Wales, was recovering from "planned abdominal surgery" she'd had the previous day at the London Clinic, an exclusive private hospital. Surgery that had been *planned*, yet no one knew about it? And, as you'll recall, they had a *planned* trip to Italy coming up.

There was immediately shock from all points on the globe. She'd be out until *Easter?* So this planned surgery was going to prevent her for months on end from showing up for five minutes and shaking some hands at one of her patronages?

And…*two weeks* in the hospital? The average person does not stay two *days* in hospital unless something's gone terribly wrong. We're talking childbirth, surgery, complications, heart attacks, you name it. Most of us are nudged out of our gurneys at the same time our IVs are being yanked out. I've had organs removed and was sent home the same day.

There were those who acted like the inconsistencies were NBD. They went on social media and talked about how life is different for the ultra-privileged, how the rich are routinely offered unusually long stays in medical facilities to recover from procedures.

Former patients at the clinic Kate Middleton was apparently treated at came out with first-person stories revealing how great the food is, how kind and pampering the medical caregivers are, how delightful the environs.

The entire situation was bizarre, but we would not be given any more context with which to process what we'd been told.

Whatever was happening, whatever the truth about Kate's ailments and location, it did not necessarily need to be known at that point. But Kensington Palace—which is William and his courtiers—set itself up for a messy winter by bungling the entire affair beyond imagination.

Chapter 9

The King is Down

Just when the shock of Kate's health news was giving way to theories, guesses, analysis and wild claims, things *really* went haywire with the British royal family.

That same day—January 17—the other court, Buckingham Palace, released its own bombshell.

Their statement dropped ninety minutes after Kensington Palace's, and it was a big one:

The reigning monarch, King Charles III, would be heading to the same hospital Kate was in.

"In common with thousands of men each year, The King has sought treatment for an enlarged prostate," the statement said. "His Majesty's condition is benign and he will attend hospital next week for a corrective procedure."

It added that the 75-year-old monarch's "public engagements will be postponed for a short period of recuperation." (Charles had been expected to attend a series of meetings and events in Scotland).

A Buckingham Palace source told NBC News that Charles "was keen to share the details of his diagnosis to encourage other men who may be experiencing symptoms to get checked, in line with public health advice."

While the world absorbed this information, Queen Camilla downplayed her husband's condition, saying on a trip to Aberdeen, Scotland that "He's fine, thank you very much. Looking forward to getting back to work."

Meanwhile, Prince William dutifully visited his ailing wife on January 18. The pressing throng of media and on-lookers outside the private London Clinic in Marylebone, the hospital where the palace said Kate was currently recovering from surgery, was treated to a view of the Prince of Wales leaving at 12:35 p.m. after a presumed morning visit with his wife. He was photographed behind the wheel of a $175,000 electric Audi E-Tron GT Carbon Vorsprong, followed by his protection team in a Range Rover.

After that sighting, it was as if Kensington Palace (William) wiped his hands and told his team, *That'll do for now.*

Because then…nothing happened.

The mainstream media, even those protective of the royal family, were left to fill an information vacuum. They sat on the London Clinic, but found it was devoid of news and notable visitors.

No sign of Kate's children. No sign of her family of origin—no Carole, Mike, no Pippa or James. William wasn't seen again; he was only spotted visiting the hospital that one time as his wife convalesced for nearly two full weeks. All very curious.

The public was on tenterhooks wondering what was going on and if the princess was truly OK, but the media could only magic up excruciating puff pieces from "sources" who said William was "clearing his diary" and was "determined" to give his children a "normal" life. We had no idea if any of that was true.

They say nature abhors a vacuum, and as Kate made nary a peep from the London Clinic and William was nowhere to be seen, you, dear reader, know what comes next: Time to make headline hash of Meghan and Harry, who the press suggested were "in hiding" as they remained out of the spotlight.

Keen readers of this series will know that if Meghan had said a word, had she stepped outside in public for any reason, she would've been hung out to dry for making Kate's hospital stay all about her. Meghan would be castigated for stealing the spotlight from poor, sick Kate. Meghan and Harry couldn't win, so they didn't try. They lived their lives.

Still, the media rambled on. Let's parse this *Page Six* headline, which surpasses the label of laughable and launches straight to ludicrous. "As royal family suffers health crises, Meghan Markle 'had no intention of pulling her weight.'"

You think I'm kidding? Nope. That was a real headline on an article published on January 20.

Can someone shoot them an email and remind them MEGHAN IS NOT A WORKING ROYAL ANYMORE? *Sigh*. She's pulling her weight in *her* life, which is *her* life, ergo it is not *your* life or the royal family's life. Unlike that family, she doesn't take a penny—not one red cent—from taxpayers in any nation. She walked down the aisle on her wedding day as a self-made millionaire and continues to support herself.

In any case, it was notable that with the top senior royals sidelined, including two of the most popular ones now based in the U.S., there was a glamour gap in the family's public-facing members. That left Prince Edward, Queen Elizabeth's youngest son, and his wife Sophie, the Duchess of Edinburgh, to take over the mantle along with Charles's sister, middle child Princess Anne. Could they do it? Good question.

A public relations disaster

Right out of the gate, Kensington Palace's handling of this crisis did more to stoke global interest in Kate's wellbeing and whereabouts than almost anything else he could've done.

This is because it started with an obvious falsehood.

When the bloody *Today Show*, NBC's anti-scandal morning program, the one that if it were a food it would be tapioca pudding smothered on soggy white toast, makes a spicy comment about the duchess's whereabouts, you know the palace is in trouble.

One bright morning in January, Savannah Guthrie asked British royal expert Daisy McAndrew in front of the *Today* show's millions of viewers, "It makes you wonder, why did you ever schedule [events] if you knew this was planned?"

Indeed, the New York *Post* alluded to the same inconsistency:

The presence of the Duke and Duchess of Sussex in the UK for this royal health crisis... may also have quelled some of the **speculation and questions over Princess Kate's condition and diagnosis, which remains unknown.**

Palace sources have been keen to stress that the surgery is not a result of cancer, but have otherwise stayed silent, and **declined to explain why they called the operation "planned" when it led to the cancellation of engagements.**

The answer is, her trip to the hospital obviously wasn't planned. Not in the way the average person thinks of planned, anyway.

Because you don't book a trip to Italy and talk to the *Daily Mail* about it if your "abdominal surgery" was "planned" in advance. To be clear, "planned" is also a word used when a surgery is not emergent, and the patient doesn't have to be rushed into the operating room. Still, those parsed medical terms raised the eyebrows of millions, including the *Today* show's own Guthrie, a lawyer and a rather intelligent woman. After all, the Italy trip was revealed December 22 and the surgery was over by January 17.

Much more transparent and easier to follow was the king's health journey as revealed by Buckingham Palace and performed by Camilla. Charles was admitted to the London Clinic, where his daughter-in-law was already settled in, on Friday, January 26. Accompanying him was Camilla, his wife and longtime love, the woman he cheated on his then-wife Princess Diana with.

As Kate continued to receive no visible visitors beyond William's one stop-by on January 18, the king had regular, public support.

Was Camilla making a point of being seen? *Hmmm.* Why would she do that? It's something to think about. Regardless, we all saw plenty of her—including on that very day.

Camilla was seen leaving the hospital hours after Charles had endured his prostate procedure, and as she headed to a waiting car, fans on stake-out outside the royal-heavy hospital called out, "We love you!"

She was back the next day, smiling for the crowd again. Charles's wife made a total of three very public visits in 24 hours.

The optics, something The Firm is all too focused on, were horrendous for Kensington Palace.

It seemed no one was visiting Kate.

Doesn't mean she has to have visitors, and if she did, she clearly doesn't have to ask them to wave to the crowd on their way out.

But it was notable that she didn't, and considering every exit and entrance was covered as a breathless press and fans from around the world staked out the hospital and the entire street and never saw any other well-known visitors, this fact raised questions.

Finally, on January 29, there was word about Kate.

And I do mean *word*. There were no sightings, no images of her, no shadow of her, a reflection of her in a blacked-out car window. With the king at the same hospital, every member of the media, influencers, looky-loos, every piece of photographic equipment from high-dollar cameras to cracked iPhones had their lenses trained on every entrance, exit, alley and back street out of that place.

We watched as King Charles and his wife, Camilla, left the London Clinic three days after his procedure. He walked out the front door, smiling and waving to concerned onlookers waiting outside the hospital.

Yet that same day, we were told via one of KP's statements, Kate also left.

Indeed, parallel statements, as if from two totally separate families, were released.

"The King was this afternoon discharged from hospital following planned medical treatment and has rescheduled forthcoming public engagements to allow for a period of private recuperation," Buckingham Palace said.

Then, "The Princess of Wales has returned home to Windsor to continue her recovery from surgery. She is making good progress," a Kensington Palace spokesperson said. "The Prince and Princess wish to say a huge thank you to the entire team at The London Clinic, especially the dedicated nursing staff, for the care they have provided. The Wales family continues to be grateful for the well wishes they have received from around the world."

But no one saw Kate that entire time. Not coming, not going. Yet suddenly, poof, she was apparently gone from the London Clinic where she was never actually seen by anyone who'd been camping outside it. The stark contrast didn't go unnoticed.

Something was rotten in Denmark.

And the world got to work trying to figure out what it was.

#WhereisKate began trending on social media, and this hashtag would be in the spotlight on and off for months.

The bombshell announcements were raining down in England that year. On February 5, the nation was shocked when Buckingham Palace revealed King Charles had been diagnosed with cancer. What kind, the palace did not say, but they did rule out prostate cancer.

Their statement revealed the king had begun "regular treatments" and would postpone public duties until it was completed. The 75-year-old remained "wholly positive about his treatment and looks forward to returning to full public duty as soon as possible," the palace added.

King Charles informed both his sons personally about his diagnosis. First William, who was nearby, and then Harry, who was a continent away. Neither William personally nor Kensington Palace made a statement about the diagnosis.

In Montecito, Harry had been following his father's health journey with some concern. Charles's initial procedure in the hospital had prompted a phone call between Harry and the king. And, Harry understood that while Charles had walked out the hospital doors with what most of us thought was the all-clear, the king was 75 years old and Harry knew there could be more challenges down the road.

The king himself called Harry days after Charles had left the London Clinic to deliver the news he'd been diagnosed with cancer. Prince Harry put down the phone and packed at great speed. Meghan would stay with the children while the prince raced to his father's side. He hopped on a plane to London faster than you could say transatlantic family reunion.

The seriousness of this diagnosis called for an in-person visit, and both father and son welcomed it.

Harry was on his hometown turf for less than 24 hours—he was pictured both coming in and going out from Heathrow airport—and he did not see his brother.

Short as it was, Prince Harry would say later how meaningful that visit was to him. "I spoke to [my father]. And I jumped on a plane and went to go see him as soon as I could," the Duke of Sussex said on *Good Morning America*. "I love my family. The fact that I was able to get on a plane, go and see him, and spend any time with him...I'm grateful for that...I've got other trips planned....so I'll stop in and see my family as much as I can."

Of course, journalists asked Harry to talk about what was said at their meeting and requested more details about his father's medical situation.

"That," Harry replied crisply, "stays between me and him."

Chapter 10

The Question Remains: #WhereIsKate?

Meanwhile, Kate was still nowhere to be seen. In early February, UK broadsheet newspaper the *Times* reported that the princess was in a medically induced coma—that is, if you believed the reporting of a Spanish journalist named Concha Calleja.

Calleja told her television show *Fiesta* that she had "spoken to an aide from the royal household in a completely off-the-record manner" and Kate's life "was in great danger." She said, in effect, that Kate was put into a medically induced coma due to "complications" during her abdominal surgery. This claim tore through social media, and it felt like there wouldn't be enough bandwidth to accommodate the number of posts and videos analyzing the latest bump in the story.

In a highly unusual move, Kensington Palace responded to the extreme claims.

Now: When a piece of "news" is coming from *one* journalist in a far off country, ignoring the wild allegations is the preferred route of royal families the world over.

So when a "palace source" came out forcefully and called Calleja's claims "total nonsense" to *The Times*, it was simply another jolt of electricity boosting the story. The source went on to say, "No attempt was made by that journalist to factcheck anything that she said with anyone in the household. It's fundamentally, totally made up, and I'll use polite English here: it's absolutely not the case."

This was more evidence to me that the show was being run by Prince William rather than an experienced comms team. More than one commentator close to the royals has said in one way or another that no one says no to Prince William. KP's moves during this time reflected an arrogance, a stubbornness, and an amateurish ditching of the royals' longtime ethos to never complain, never explain.

Robert Jobson, once dubbed the godfather of royal reporting by the *Wall Street Journal*, used long sentences to dance around the point without actually saying it: No one tells William no. Quoting a "source in the royal household," Jobson wrote in the *Daily Mail* when William was in his mid-thirties that "the Duke of Cambridge has some very good, innovative ideas. But the Duke can be a little unforgiving. When he gets it right everyone is patting him on the back, but who is there to criticise him and warn against getting it wrong?"

The implication is clear: No one is.

Added Jobson, "At Kensington Palace, a dedicated but notably youthful group of advisers is slavishly loyal to the boss."

By February 29, the tsunami of speculation was so ferocious that Kensington Palace came out of nowhere to try to tamp down the rising tide of *#WhereIsKate?*

KP released a rather irritable statement (William, is that you?) and slammed the public for worrying about Kate's health and, let's face it, William's handling of the situation.

"We were very clear from the outset that the Princess of Wales was out until after Easter and Kensington Palace would only be providing updates when something was significant," a spokesperson for Princess Kate said.

Problem was, they were lying again.

Before I get into trouble for using the L word, read on, and then tell me why this isn't a lie: They said they'd be providing updates about her wellbeing when "something was significant"—and something very significant *had* indeed happened (more below) and they were *not* offering any updates.

If something huge happens and you don't want to reveal it, then say that. Don't say you're sharing news "when it's significant." Say, you're sharing news "when we're ready."

Still with me?

You can absolutely protect someone's privacy without lying. Why hadn't they figured out yet that misleading doesn't work, so why do it? Kensington Palace's credibility was eroding statement by statement, day by day, image by image, while Buckingham Palace was striking the balance between privacy and public relations with the king's cancer.

Entertainment industry bible *The Hollywood Reporter* put out a story in light of that statement, flicking at what was prompting the rampant speculation, essentially giving a nod to the fact that *of course* we were all confused and concerned: "Rumors grew louder over the next several weeks and…more fodder for speculation came when Prince William pulled out of a memorial service in Windsor to honor King Constantine of Greece, his godfather; 'a personal matter' was the reason given for this sudden move, so naturally, royal watchers' thoughts turned to Catherine and her ongoing recovery," THR wrote.

If you're reading this in the distant future and weren't following the royal drama that winter, know that it was a genuinely unnerving time; there was a sense of foreboding, and there was absolute concern for the princess. It was a spooky feeling to be told various stories about where she was at a given time without ever seeing her, despite the pressing media hordes who do, let's face it, manage to snap their subjects when they really, really want to.

Spring has sprung

March eased in, leaving February in its dust. Kensington Palace was still flailing. Statements weren't working. William out doing engagements on his own was making things worse. The world wouldn't stop asking *#WhereisKate?*

It was time for a photo to prove Kate was OK.

Problem was, the one that emerged wasn't the kind of image Kensington Palace ever would have wanted out there.

Keep in mind the king had announced he had cancer, and was still out and about waving at people. We knew where he was. No one outside Kate's small circle truly knew where she was. A lot of people were very, very concerned for her.

And then stuff hit the fan.

On March 4, a picture emerged that would shock the world. American online scandal sheet TMZ ran a photo in which a woman they identified as Princess Kate was "riding passenger in a vehicle that was being driven by her mother, Carole, near Windsor Castle in the UK...and like we said, this sighting is a big deal considering we haven't seen her whatsoever since December."

The most notable thing about this alleged first look at Kate out of the hospital was that none of the UK media picked the image up. This tells you a lot; for one, it tells you they knew Kensington Palace would be furious at them if they ran it. It suggests they didn't know if it really was Kate or not. Or, it meant they knew for certain it *was* Kate, and for legal reasons—we know it wouldn't be ethics stopping them—they chose to err on the side of not invading her privacy.

If you Google the image, you'll see that if it was Kate—*if*—her appearance had drastically changed. The face of the person in the image was puffy, a different shape, and had different facial features than the Kate we're used to seeing. I'll leave readers to make up their own minds about this image, and when you go to research it, you'll find people suggesting many things, including that there were too many wheels on the Audi, so they suspected the image was altered, or that the woman was actually Kate's sister, Pippa, standing in for her; and many other observations. I do not put stock in or necessarily agree with any of the above. But that is some of what social media was chattering about.

While the royals in England were doing their thing, Harry and Meghan were keeping a watchful eye on events back home while continuing to honor the commitments they each had. Meghan had a soft launch of her new brand to worry about, but as always, she was keeping abreast of her favorite causes.

On March 8, she was the keynote speaker on a high-profile panel marking International Women's Day at the annual SXSW festival in Austin, Texas. Meghan's panel was titled Breaking Barriers, Shaping Narratives: How Women Lead On And Off The Screen, and she spoke candidly to a room full of people sympathetic with her experience with online abuse.

As Prince Harry sat in the front row nodding along, Meghan revealed the personal pain the couple has experienced from toxic online attacks.

She said she now avoids reading any of it as much as possible for her own wellbeing, and said she believed people have "forgotten our humanity" when it comes to media, both social and mainstream.

"The bulk of the bullying and abuse that I was experiencing on social media and online was when I was pregnant with Archie and with Lili," she told the crowd. "You just think about that and really wrap your head around why people would be so hateful—it is not catty, it is cruel."

Chapter 11

A Mother's Day Debacle & a Farmstand Fiasco

A few days later, Kensington Palace released a photo to mark Mother's Day in the UK. The image instantly made history, but not the kind of history Kensington Palace was trying to make.

The image showed Kate with tumbling locks and the bright, dimply smile we're used to, with no trace of the person we saw in the TMZ photo mere days earlier. In it, she's surrounded by her children, George, Charlotte and Louis.

Here was the first alarm bell: Kensington Palace released the photo to news agencies and on social media and told the world it was taken by Prince William *earlier that week at the family's home in Windsor.* Many found that difficult to believe.

After the photo was shared with the public, viewers began to suggest the image of Kate and the kids was heavily edited, or possibly even AI-generated. News agencies worldwide—including the Associated Press, Getty Images,

Reuters and the AFP—agreed. They pulled the photo from distribution, citing concerns about manipulation.

The AP swiftly issued a "kill notification" to its clients, writing in an alert to journalists that after "closer inspection it appears that the source has manipulated the image. No replacement photo will be sent." The AP cited the inconsistency in the alignment of Princess Charlotte's left hand as one reason to pull it. Outside observers also noticed inconsistencies in the alignment of the sweater pattern on Prince Louis's shoulder and a jagged white line in the background near his knee.

Wrote ITV royal reporter Chris Ship, "No comment from Kensington Palace tonight after at least 3 international pictures agencies refuse to distribute this morning's photo of Kate and her children."

It wasn't over yet. Getty Images also flagged a photograph Kate had taken of the late Queen Elizabeth II alongside her grandchildren and great-grandchildren in the summer of 2022, adding an editor's note that said this photo "has been digitally enhanced at source."

The literal entire world took the Waleses to the cleaners for the Mother's Day photo. Hell, even Instagram flagged it as problematic. I urge you to read comments from experts who carefully analyzed the image and found plenty of messed-up photoshopping.

Not sure what a big deal this is? Think of it this way: Never in the history of the world has a stalwart news agency like the Associated Press put a kill order on a photograph released from the British royal family.

Not once.

Not ever.

Let that sink in.

We were in uncharted waters, and Kate was still nowhere to be seen.

Still, anyone questioning her whereabouts and wellbeing was met with anonymous online outrage about how any questions about Kate were by definition invasive and wrong. *She's not missing! We know where she is. They told us! She's at Windsor! Leave her alone!*

Wrong. We knew by then that KP is not above releasing misleading information and images. As those of us who understood how unprecedented this strategy was would reply—if we responded at all—*We're not bothering Kate. We're questioning William.*

(Could some of those defending KP's actions online have been bots hired by the palace itself? The New York *Times* in 2020 suggested, after a deep investigation, there was evidence KP's Instagram accounts might be buying followers).

Anyway, someone was going to have to answer for that photograph.

It didn't take long for someone in the royal family to be the one to fall on their sword.

We hadn't heard anything from Kate directly throughout all of this. She was busy recovering and hopefully healing, as far as we knew. But suddenly, Kensington Palace decided the world *had* to hear her voice, and the chosen moment was when there was blame to be taken. It would be the woman without royal blood, the mother of three young children, a woman who was suffering in ways we still hadn't been fully briefed on.

"Like many amateur photographers, I do occasionally experiment with editing," Kate allegedly wrote on X, formerly known as Twitter, on March 11. "I wanted to express my apologies for any confusion the family photograph we shared yesterday caused."

This only exacerbated things. Social media erupted. *What was William thinking?*

To either encourage, force, or allow—we do not know which it was—your very ill wife to take the blame for an action that put a dent in the credibility of an institution, an action it seemed like the entire world was currently focusing on, was…something.

It was about to get worse.

The famous farm shop affair took the mess Kensington Palace had cooked up and splattered it against the wall.

It was a pleasant spring day when the tabloids reported there was a sighting! *A real sighting!* The elusive royal couple, towering William and lithe Kate, were fine—in fact, they were having a lovely Saturday together perusing petunias and ears of corn at a local farm shop near their Windsor home.

Intriguing, right?

The *Daily Beast*, a decidedly royals-friendly publication, reported on the moment this way: "Tabloid stories about the sighting of the recently reclusive royal were oddly devoid of any photographic proof," the article said. "Royal fans, well-wishers, and the growing contingent of conspiracy theorists wildly speculating about Kate's disappearance from the public eye since undergoing abdominal surgery late last year [sic] just had to take their word for it."

Or did they? The message, apparently, was heard loud and clear.

Wouldn'tcha know it, by Monday, a video documenting this "sighting" miraculously appeared!

This one emerged March 18. It was a 38-second grainy video taken from afar and appeared to show two people that looked a bit like Prince William and Kate Middleton striding purposefully out of the aforementioned farm shop toward the parking lot. The woman is carrying what looks like a fairly substantial shopping bag. For someone with recent major abdominal surgery, that seemed like a lot of activity. I do know that my husband would've carried my bag for me with his free hand. In the video, the man who resembles Prince William has a free hand.

TMZ and *The Sun* tossed the clip out there in tandem, alongside identical quotes from the onlooker who apparently shot the video. Neither publication mentioned the odd delay between the sighting and the evidence provided to support said sighting.

As someone who has covered, met and interviewed celebrities for decades—one of my first was John F. Kennedy Jr., one I'll never forget—I can tell you that the most sought-after and talked-about woman on planet earth is not going to stroll out unnoticed, unhindered, at a farm shop. Every iPhone camera in the area would be out faster than you could say summer squash. Yet the people sitting around them as they race by are not even looking up, and to date only that one video has come out. When the royals are around, there are conspicuous Range Rovers and protection officers onsite (again, I've been around Will and Kate. It's a scene). If the people in the video were lookalikes, whether coincidentally hanging out together at a farmstand or positioned there as a set-up, there wouldn't have to be an entourage.

Was it a set-up?

I don't know. What I do know is the British tabloids are *incredibly* skilled at finding people who were at a given event or place at a given time, offering them cash, and getting them to talk. And yet not a single additional onlooker at the shop that day came forward and provided their name. The man who recorded the pair swore he was really there and caught them on film and called anyone questioning if it was Kate in the video "delusional."

"Some even refused to believe our front page yesterday," *The Sun* sniffed in its follow-up article, noting that "vile and bullying online behavior" targeting the royals was running rampant.

Sorry, folks, but questioning a tabloid that's been caught up in numerous court cases and settlements related to reporting false stories, including phone hacking and libel, is a very normal thing to do.

The Sun also said they showed the video to Kensington Palace before publishing. That means they at least had KP's tacit permission to run with it.

And yet Kate's own spokesperson over at Kensington Palace never said it was her in the video. The *Daily Beast* tried to authenticate it, but the reporter said Kate's office, when asked if she was farm stand lady, "said they wouldn't comment on her private time."

Therein lies a major clue. There is no need to abuse people who don't see Kate in the thin brunette woman on our screens, because Kate herself hasn't said it was her.

This is not a conspiracy theory. This is a difference of opinion, a variation in how our eyes work and our brains perceive things, and a lot of us do not see Kate Middleton in that photo. Others do. It's not a "conspiracy theory" to examine a grainy, distant video presented to us by two scandal sheets and not see Kate or William in it.

Kate herself **has not said that was her** in the video. Therefore, why should we feel pressured to believe it is?

TMZ, which ran the video as a Kate sighting, backtracked quickly, with at least one of their staff saying publicly they believed there's every chance that *wasn't* Kate in the video. Having covered royals for a long time and been around Kate in private, knowing her gait, her way of smiling but always letting it drop after a short time while this woman did *not*, plus the length of her legs, her ears, her chin…it's simply not Kate.

I'm with American reality TV personality Andy Cohen, who said flatly, "That ain't Kate."

"It's so far gone and so out of control that some people aren't going to believe anything now," one skeptic wrote on Reddit alongside many posters who simply shrugged and said, *I have no dog in this fight, but that doesn't look like Kate or William.* "To be honest, I don't know what they were all thinking going from 'she's extremely unwell and unable to appear at any events or in any photos' to 'oh she's skipping about smiling and shopping.' That was never going to go down well."

It didn't.

Whomever approved it or whomever is in it, the bizarre sequence of events and the video itself made things worse. "At this point," another royal observer wrote, "if KP said the sky was blue, I'd look up and halfway expect to see green. Something unusual must have happened to make their PR act so oddly, and until KP clears the air on that, they won't regain trust."

What we didn't know was that decisions had already been made at high levels that would change everything.

Chapter 12

Getting out of Hand

The mainstream media were now fully invested and were acknowledging something was rotten in England. In a March 19 CBS national news broadcast, one that is as mainstream as it gets, the newsreader acknowledged "the controversy over [Kate's] extended absence from the public eye…has only gotten worse."

American reality TV personality Andy Cohen asked John Oliver on the former's show, "I have to ask you—what the *fuck* is going on with *Kate Middleton*?" There's much more. It just kept going.

And then, out of nowhere, the *Daily Mail* ran an article that steered chatter in a different direction. The article quoted royal author Robert Lacey and focused on William's anger issues. "In the years after her 2005 marriage to Prince Charles, Camilla recounted to members of her own family and close friends her surprise at discovering this unexpected side to Prince Charming—'The boy's got a temper!'

"Charles's wife was horrified at the ranting and raving that William unleashed on occasion against her husband in her presence. The rows were shattering, by Camilla's account in the early days, with William doing the shouting and Charles submitting meekly on the receiving end. As she described it, William held nothing back."

American women's website SheKnows picked up on this, running a story headlined, "Prince William's Reported Hot Temper Is Getting a Second Glance by British Tabloids."

The article went on to say, "It seems that the *Daily Mail* is giving William's temper a second look. They took a deep dive into Robert Lacey's royal biography, *Battle of Brothers*, where the author also chronicled the Prince of Wales's reputation for being hot-headed.

"These stories are seeing the light of day again, and it almost feels like a warning shot to Prince William from the British tabloids. Is the Royal Rota no longer protecting him and his image? That's sure how it feels as the tide has turned against Kensington Palace's PR blunder in handling Kate Middleton's health crisis. There appears to be a much different tone to the headlines lately, and it doesn't bode well for the royal family, particularly Prince William."

Same day, celebrity blog *Celebitchy* observed, "The real question is: why are they bringing this up again right now? In the first edition of the book, [author Robert] Lacey was quite critical of William, leaving enough breadcrumbs to reveal that Huevo [a nickname for Prince William in royal-critical circles] has always been a rage-monster who flies off the handle (sometimes violently) often. Lacey also made it clear, in the original version, that William was incandescent with rage and jealousy towards Harry, that William did everything to 'edge out' his brother, and on and on."

Prince Harry wrote of his brother's rages in his memoir *Spare*, saying a verbal spat grew physical when William hurled an insult at his brother, then lunged at him.

As Harry tells it, "It all happened so fast. So very fast. He grabbed me by the collar, ripping my necklace, and he knocked me to the floor. I landed on the dog's bowl, which cracked under my back, the pieces cutting into me. I lay there for a moment, dazed, then got to my feet and told him to get out."

William taunted Harry, urging him to hit back like they'd done as children. Harry didn't.

William abruptly left and, after taking a moment to gather himself, came back inside "looking regretful, and apologized," Harry would later explain.

Eventually his brother headed out again, but as he did, William "turned and called back: 'You don't need to tell Meg about this.'"

"You mean that you attacked me?" Harry replied.

"I didn't attack you, Harold," William reportedly replied.

Harry called his therapist instead of telling his wife, but later, when Meghan inevitably noticed the "scrapes and bruises" on his back, Harry confessed all about the attack.

Meghan, too, had been faced with an angry heir getting in her face.

Harry wrote in *Spare* that during an odd conversation about Meghan apparently offending Kate, "Kate's eyes widened: 'Yes. You talked about my hormones. We're not close enough for you to talk about my hormones!'

"Meg's eyes got wide too. She looked genuinely confused. 'I'm sorry I talked about your hormones. That's just how I talk with my girlfriends.'"

Harry then claims that "Willy" stepped in and "pointed at Meg."

"'It's rude, Meghan. It's not what's done here in Britain,'" William reportedly said.

To which Meghan apparently replied: "Kindly take your finger out of my face."

Perhaps more chilling still is William allegedly got physical with his own mother, Princess Diana, according to that same *Mail* article about Lacey's reporting: "The anger had been apparent from early on, notably when his mother, Diana, had appeared in a 1995 Panorama interview with the now disgraced Martin Bashir."

William was not happy about the interview, the *Mail* goes on to say, and "Diana soon felt the full force." Diana allegedly told a friend that "all hell broke loose" and William was shouting and crying, and when she tried to put her arms around him, he shoved her away.

"Diana was getting a taste of how William's intensity could lead to his notorious rages. The following day, he apologised to his mother for his temper with a small bunch of flowers," Lacey wrote, according to the *Mail*.

You can see William's temper for yourself if you head over to YouTube. Search for Prince William + Flying into rage + photographer ("berating" will also bring up results). I will also link to it on my Substack newsletter, *Everything is a Mystery*. Warning: It may be triggering for some people. William is imposing, accusatory, and breathless with rage. This is a video of the prince getting in the face of and unleashing on a man who was on public land, who swore he was *not* walking there to try to take photos of the family, who remained calm as he was verbally attacked, and who denied repeatedly that he'd gone anywhere near William and Kate's home.

William is spitting mad; he is incandescent in the video. Now, like his brother Harry, he's had a traumatic past with paparazzi and a righteous anger at their invasive ways since he was a child. But the man he spoke to like he was garbage was not a part of that pack, from what I can find online.

It's important to note we still don't know the full story of that day and what the man's goal was, as the photographer hasn't come forward to discuss it.

Just as these articles emerged, the most important royal video of the year dropped.

When it came out, the world stopped. Kensington Palace released it wide as they had with the Mother's Day photo.

It showed Kate Middleton sitting alone on a bench inside what appeared to be a set with a static, meadow-like background. We were told it was created by "BBC Studios," which is not a news organization. It is a "content company" that puts out everything from podcasts to Dr. Who and other fictional programs.

Kate sat alone on a bench and told the world what she'd been struggling through.

"In January, I underwent major abdominal surgery in London, and at the time, it was thought that my condition was non-cancerous," she said. "The surgery was successful. However, tests after the operation found cancer had been present. My medical team therefore advised that I should undergo a course of preventative chemotherapy, and I am now in the early stages of that treatment."

She said it was "a huge shock," and that she and Prince William "have been doing everything we can to process and manage this privately for the sake of our young family. As you can imagine, this has taken time. It has taken me time to recover from major surgery in order to start my treatment.

"But, most importantly, it has taken us time to explain everything to George, Charlotte and Louis in a way that is appropriate for them, and to reassure them that I am going to be OK."

"Having William by my side is a great source of comfort and reassurance too," she added, though William was not by her side when she said this.

She asked for privacy, and we learned that the chemotherapy began in late February, though no one revealed what type of cancer she had.

As well wishes poured in from around the world—I personally had just made an appointment at a top cancer hospital for a second opinion on my potential malignancy and had great empathy for her—there were still questions from people whose trust in KP was dwindling.

Given the seriousness of Kate's revelation, there was continued analysis by a shocked public about the weirdness surrounding everything to do with it. Once again, KP had bungled the delivery of this most sensitive message, and it left people with lingering questions about what was going on inside the royal family.

First, a legendary agency whose reputation is beyond reproach, Getty, flagged the video for its clients, labeling it as content that "may not adhere to Getty Images' editorial policy."

It is a fact that Getty does not do this for every "third-party handout" (as opposed to content created by their own teams), and that this label was slapped on KP's video for a reason.

However, when there was an uproar over KP apparently sending out yet more possibly manipulated or even faked content, Getty responded by saying such a label is normal for third-party handouts.

Yet that same week, there were several "third-party handouts" coming from Getty that did *not* have that cautionary label, including an image of a Jonas Brother in Greece. So we were left to think that maybe, after all, there might be something off about the new video.

The quality of the video itself is unusual, to be sure: It's gauzy, dreamy, and a bit shaky in places. Experts found glitching pixels and pointed out a bizarre effect wherein it looks like Kate has an extra row of bottom teeth, for just two examples. Before long, an AI firm ran a check on the video and pronounced there was a high likelihood it was AI generated—it was probably a deepfake and *not* the actual Kate Middleton. However, multiple other respected experts in the field disagreed, and said they firmly believed it was real. From there, the mainstream vibe was one of: *Kate's not well, that's her in the video, time to support her and let it go.*

If we accept the video was 100% real and on the up-and-up, we're left with the visuals its creator wanted us to see. And the most striking thing about it? The aloneness of Kate's brave stand.

We were being asked to believe what both William and Kate were *telling* us, and to ignore what we were *seeing*.

This is something those in power often do, and if you question the party line, you're invasive; a troublemaker; a hater. We were *told* William was by his wife's side through it all, that he was a rock standing firm with her. We didn't *see* that. We saw him in a car one time leaving the hospital where we were told Kate was staying for two weeks.

Then, we *saw* Kate alone on a bench telling the world about one of the worst things that has ever happened to her. William was nowhere to be found. Why wouldn't the prince and his princess sit together and face the camera in a show of unity that Charles and Camilla were all too happy to display? Why didn't Wiliam and Kate *show* the world what they are all too happy to keep *telling* us, that they are getting through this *together*?

This is the crux of what I believe caused the meltdown of Kensington Palace's communications that season.

I believe Kate was no longer complying.

In my opinion, she wasn't up for being photographed, so she didn't allow it. I imagine Kate simply did not want to be seen in public in the same way us mortals do when we're not feeling our best. How often do we think to ourselves, *I'm not fit to be seen at the supermarket*? Except there aren't millions of people waiting with bated breath for us to be caught in leggings and an unwashed topknot coming out of Sainsbury's or Kroger.

I believe Kate didn't agree to a happy-clappy photo session or a pap stroll (where a celebrity tips off a favored paparazzo to capture a "sighting" of them in public; this is something celebrities the world over participate in), and that left William in a bind.

He was still ostensibly "working," and he had to face down the pressure of the questions the world was throwing out there about Kate's well-being.

King Charles and Camilla proved it could be done, that a balance could be struck between privacy and transparency, but something prevented KP from doing that.

There were two factors at play, I believe. One is the fact Kate refused to play ball, in my opinion. Everything KP said and did that season smacked of a one-man show, not of teamwork. We were told there was unity, but we saw the opposite. Kate alone took the blame for the photo. Kate alone sat on that bench. Kate, if it was truly her, was with her mother in that TMZ car photo, not with William.

And as pressure mounted on the prince, I believe he was directing the PR strategy, and his team *was* complying, whether William's ideas were good or not. Who's there to tell him no? I'm not sure there's anyone.

Whether the final video is AI or not, whether it's 100% real or slightly tweaked, Kate sitting alone on a bench was a stark message.

The firm knows better than anyone about optics.

I believe Kate did it her way.

Message received.

Eventually, the royal family returned to an equilibrium of sorts, and Kate appeared alive and well, coming back smiling at the Wimbledon men's final in July (she's rarely or never seen at the women's final), and wowing fans with her fashion choices.

So here's the question: Did any of that drama have to happen at all?

No, it didn't. But there were reasons it spiraled so out of the royal family's control, and it remains to be seen if they've learned anything from it at all.

PART III:

Launch of The Jam Offensive

Chapter 13

The Sussex Invasion

My dearest Mary,

I write to you from the trenches of the last jam stand. Barrels of boiling fruit are flying thick and fast, and I don't know how much time I have. King Charles the Cruel has put an embargo on the last reserves of preserves.

If our rations hold out long enough to see this worthy battle through, my darling, I will live to hold you once again. There is talk of sabotaging the enemy's glorious strawberry supplies with rancid rhubarb—because who actually likes rhubarb, let's be honest—but I suspect the Duchess is far too crafty to allow that. We ride at dawn.

All my love,
John

In the chronicle of the Sussex Age, the spring of 2024 shall forever be known as the dawn of the Great Jam Wars. A member of the British royal family by the name of Meghan, the Duchess of Sussex, who had brashly and brazenly set up a rival court in the United States of America, fired the first salvo.

It was a devastating cannonade, to be sure. Her husband, the Duke of Sussex, was known to be a supportive spouse and able ally in the new offensive. With news of the duchess's opening chess move, warring factions emerged, ready to take up virtual arms in support of the House of Sussex.

The declaration of war was made on April 15 with the launching of the Sussex Jam Offensive on United States soil. It began when, like sleeper cells activated on command, one by one, a high-profile person received a coded message and dutifully rose up to signal the battle was *on*.

First to reveal themselves as allies of the devious duchess were designer Tracy Robbins and model-slash-businesswoman Delfina Blaquier, two women of some means and accomplishment who are both married to well-known men.

That cool day in April, Tracy and Delfina took a stand and defiantly shared photos on social media of small-batch strawberry jam that clearly came from a gift basket sent by the duchess.

"Thank you, M," Tracy Robbins controversially wrote, clearly with no thought to how such words would affect the subjects of jam-starved Great Britan across the ocean. "Thank you for the delicious basket! I absolutely love this jam so not sure I'm sharing with anyone!"

Robbins' incendiary words were placed provocatively next to a picture of Meghan's blood-red jam, upon which was penned the intriguing code: "17 of 50."

It was *on.*

Ye Olde *Daily Mael* trumpeted the onset of the conflict, writing, "The royal battle of the jams has officially begun!"

What, pray tell, prompted said battle?

"Sources close to the Sussexes have stressed Meghan's jam is as authentic as it comes, amid sales of her father-in-law's similar product enjoying a spike in sales," the newspaper reported.

The duchess did not intend to let up. She sent a basket of lemons and a jar of jam to actor, writer and business-woman Mindy Kaling, who had gotten to know the Sussexes after she appeared with Prince Harry at a business conference. Like a loyal foot soldier, Kaling posted a photo of the gift basket on her IG stories with one subversive word: "OBSESSED."

Her unique code was also there for all to see: "19 of 50."

The brazen posts by these women, who are heretofore known as "jamfluencers," represented the enemy's first peek at a top-secret endeavour by the duchess, one that was said to be bestowed with the title of American Riviera Orchard.

Meanwhile, the reigning monarch, King Charles III, who some subjects had taken to calling King Charles the

Cruel on the Social Medias for reasons we shall address in due time, gathered his courtiers to plan a counteroffensive.

Why, you ask? For the monarch himself had been selling jams himself for many years! The American duchess's rival fruit spread was an affront to the nation of Great Britain.

One of the king's allies, royal brown-noser Richard Eden, a columnist for a British tabloid, wrote of Meghan's entrepreneurship in one of his diaries, "While profits from Meghan's business endeavours go to herself, any excess money made as part of the Highgrove brand is donated to charity."

Is the money donated, though, Richard? How can we be sure? And if so, how much goes to charity? Highgrove is part of the Duchy of Cornwall, whose finances are not fully transparent. Furthermore, the king's domain, the Duchy of Lancaster, allegedly skims money from dead subjects, if you believe the British news organization known as *The Guardian*.

Duchess Meghan, some angry British people were complaining, was out of line and vulgar for producing a fruit-based product and selling it for money, instead of giving it away to the whole world for free. But King Charles III, who was charging his fruit-loving British subjects ten bucks a jar in the year 2024, was *not* vulgar or out of line.

Which is it, handwringers of Great Britain? Is it cool to sell overpriced branded jam, or isn't it? And where are the reports that show *all* of King Charles III's food profits go to charity?

As the battle wore on, much was at stake. The culture wars between the Pernicious Preserves Perpetrators and the Anti-Jam Faction reached its boiling point, with *The Telegraph* newspaper taking a stand against the duchess's attempt to sell condiments.

The paper's Ed Cumming wrote, "What enriches her will make customers poor and miserable, which isn't much of a lifestyle."

He explained Duchess Meghan's apparent new brand, American Riviera Orchard, is "absurdly named," and added that "yoga mats" are on the list of Meghan's crimes, predicting she might very well try to sell these through her new company—to the detriment of society.

"No matter how many yoga mats you buy, you'll never look like Meghan," Ed proclaimed.

Wait—I won't? That's *it*. I give up! If I can't look like Meghan Markle Sussex, why live? Why do anything? Why bother with self-improvement and self-care? Where did you go to journalism school, Ed? How could a 5' 9" white woman like me hope that jam and yoga would transform me into a younger, petiter, mixed-race woman called Meghan? Are you OK?

Record scratch.

Let's unpack the jam situation in more modern lingo.

The reality is, as followers and fans of the Sussex family will know, the Great Jam Wars weren't actually so great.

They were entirely pointless, as attacks on Meghan usually are.

We sometimes use humor here at the *Harry & Meghan* biography series to lighten the mood and shed light on the absurdity of how internet trolls operate from behind their keyboards.

In this spirit, we travel forward now to the modern-day world and explain what happened.

Here's how Jamgate went down.

On March 14, the world woke up to a brand-spanking-new Instagram account for a mysterious entity called American Riviera Orchard. The account posted one Instagram "story"—essentially a short video—and it showed the duchess herself in a beige-y kitchen in a white tank top.

The American Riviera Orchard account was revealing, as it turned out, the soft launch of a new brand.

The name, no doubt a mouthful, was carefully chosen to be unique and to capture the vibe of a clean, classy, feel-good brand. Meghan made a point of invoking her current hometown of Montecito, which is part of Santa Barbara County.

"Santa Barbara has been fondly referred to as 'The American Riviera' for more than a century because of its temperate climate and lush landscapes, as well as its robust food and wine culture," *Travel & Leisure* magazine wrote of that region's chic nickname.

Meghan already had been working on the brand for some time before revealing what fans had quickly dubbed ARO for short. She and/or her team filed trademark applications for the brand in February of 2023 and indicated she'd be dipping her toes in several different product arenas: cookbooks, tableware, coffee and tea services, jellies, jams, tablecloths, cookbooks, serving ware, cutlery, spreads of all kinds, and lots more.

To kick off her new venture as a homefluencer, Meghan began making and sending out jams. Nothing controversial, right?

You're not new here, so you know the answer is that a controversy *was* coming, not just about the production of the jam itself, but about the friends Meghan chose to send her inaugural batch to.

Here's the thing about high-profile people: what the average person sees in them is generally what the celebrities want to show you. I've only encountered a few famous folks who let the mask slip in front of me.

The two worst of all time were Hilary Swank and Gordon Ramsay. While Jon Bon Jovi was a close third, he didn't spend as much time being cruel to me as the other two. I have Ramsay recorded on the night he, along with his wife Tana, sneered and mocked me at Elton John's Oscars party for simply asking how they were doing. The tape is still hard to listen to. Hilary was a flat-out mean girl sitting next to me at a gala dinner.

Then again, Harvey Weinstein was nice to me, so you catch my drift; can you ever truly know a person, especially one you've met once or twice? There are a lot of fakes out there, and a lot of people hiding behind masks.

By and large, how a famous person treats you in a particular moment is but a slice of who they are as a person. A celebrity knows they're being watched, scrutinized, copied, recorded. They're well trained in how to present themselves to leave us with a positive impression, and with positive things to say about them.

Let's take Chrissy Teigen, a friend of Meghan's, as an example of a complicated and layered character.

When I met Chrissy at a gala in New York City, we talked about internet bullying, particularly towards women. She remains one of my favorite people to interview: approachable, funny, authentic, open. At the time, around 2014, she was being trolled heavily for—and I am going to be deliberately vague here so as not to spread the cruelty trolls thrive on—being a beautiful swimsuit model who didn't match *every single human person's* idea of female bodily perfection on a given day.

I asked Chrissy if the criticism was affecting her, because her online persona was all about quips, clap-backs and throwaway barbs.

Her eyes widened and her arms went up. "Yes," she said. "*Yes.*"

Sometimes the online abuse got to her; other times she'd laugh it off, she explained.

"It's [usually] funny to me, but sometimes when you're having a bad day, it's hurtful," she says. "You just never know."

Like many of us who've faced internet trolling, her feelings about strangers' attacks are complex. It's easy to tell victims of cyberbullying to let it go. *Just block and ignore! They don't matter.* But when they come at you all day every day with vile language you'd never hear or speak in real life, it affects you. And if your brand, your work, your career, depends on sharing your life on social media, where does that leave you?

Which brings us to how Chrissy Teigen made a big splash as an ARO jam recipient. She took the strawberry preserves Meghan gifted her and concocted a mouth-watering recipe, revealing it in a video as she smothered the jam on sourdough, added soft cheese, and turned it into a delectable sandwich.

But there were vociferous people who weren't as impressed by the food as they were disgusted that Teigen was given a gift basket and a jar of jam. Why, you ask?

Because Teigen was called out in 2021 for a slew of old, mean social media posts. Some of them were ugly and damaging, particularly some she sent to a teenaged celebrity. As we all know, cyberbullying is a behavior that Meghan and Harry have both come out strongly against—and it's one Chrissy herself has been the target of.

She was duly punished at the time, buried under social-media pile-ons and losing sponsorships and deals; her wares were soon scrubbed from Target's website, for example.

Ouch, right?

So how do we square this nice, sweet, mean, bullied *and* bullying woman with the one who calls herself a friend of Duchess Meghan and Prince Harry?

There's a key word that is also a part of the Sussex arsenal: *Forgiveness*. Maybe Chrissy's heartfelt public *and* apparent private apologies to those she'd harmed moved Meghan. Maybe she, Chrissy, along with many of us out there, had grown up a bit in the past few years.

As Meghan once said, "I think forgiveness is really important. It takes a lot more energy to not forgive."

Several things can be true at once. Harry and Meghan have made it clear they're *very* careful about who enters their inner circle. Said one close source, "They surround themselves with loyal friends and are very cautious about who they invite into their lives. Meghan is very focused on building a great network. She is the type of person who will not only remember your birthday, she'll also send a very personal and thoughtful gift."

Meghan, of course, was slammed on social media for daring to collaborate with Chrissy.

She knew that would happen.

She did it anyway.

Whatever your views of Chrissy Teigen are now, she and Meghan are both members of a club no one wants to join, one too many of us belong to: Women who have had miscarriages. That searing sisterhood appears to have transcended past mistakes.

Both Chrissy and Meghan suffered miscarriages in 2020, and in Meghan's case, she shared her pain, loss and healing journey in an article she wrote for the New York *Times*.

And then the duchess reached out to another woman who had shared her experience publicly: Chrissy Teigen.

"She's been so kind to me ever since we connected," Chrissy said of Meghan in 2021 on the TV talk show *Watch What Happens Live*. "She had written me about baby Jack and loss. She is really wonderful, and just as kind as everyone says she is. That's why you look at everything and you're like 'My god, what is absolutely wrong with people that they have to make this person out to be so malicious or so crazy?'"

But criticism of Meghan's jam-loving friends was not the war; that was simply another battle.

The jammy drama across the pond was stirred up when news got out that certain British people were so offended by Meghan making jam that they opened their wallets to put her in her place.

Not long after Meghan's jamfluencers began sharing the gifts she'd sent them on social media, King Charles's Highgrove Organic Strawberry Preserves, a brand formerly known as Duchy Originals, sold out. This product is described on Highgrove's Web site as "a mouth-watering combination of plump ripe strawberries and tangy lemon."

Sounds delicious. But what was with the timing of its selling out? Easy: Pure hatred.

"That's right," wrote *New York* magazine's the *Cut*, "there are Brits so cranky that they bought Charles's jam out of spite."

Indeed, King Charles and Duchess Meghan living their respective lives with inadvertently dueling fruit products were a topic of hot debate the world over.

But here's the thing: There were some important points brought up by certain media outlets.

The royal family's riches

Often, royalists will loudly proclaim that King Charles's Duchy of Lancaster money goes back to the people, and they get quite cross if you dare say these funds enrich the king or the royal family in general.

Problem is, this money *absolutely does go into the royal family's coffers*, says the *Guardian* newspaper, which exposed an alleged sleazy side to the murky dealings behind the king's billion(s).

According to the newspaper's investigation, "The Duchy of Lancaster, a controversial land and property estate that generates huge profits for King Charles III, has collected tens of millions of pounds in recent years under an antiquated system that dates back to feudal times."

What? That is a strong statement. But their reporters came with receipts, and they revealed that the king is profiting off dead subjects. You read that right:

"Financial assets known as *bona vacantia*, owned by **people who died without a will or known next of kin**, are collected by the duchy," the *Guardian* writes. "Over the last 10 years, it has collected more than £60m in the funds. It has long claimed that, after deducting costs, *bona vacantia* revenues are donated to charities."

And then they drop a bombshell: "*However, only a small percentage of these revenues is being given to charity.*"

This is an important point to make, because Meghan is trying to make a living and not living off any taxpayers, yet she's criticized.

Meanwhile, King Charles III and other royals are congratulated for making jam and selling it...while living, in part, off of British taxpayers.

The *Guardian* goes on to say the king's Duchy is "using revenues collected from dead citizens to refurbish its profitable property portfolio, making considerable savings for the estate. One said duchy insiders regarded the *bona vacantia* expenditure, which has **until now not been publicly disclosed, as akin to 'free money' and a 'slush fund'...The diversion of *bona vacantia* funds in this way has proven a financial boon to the king's estate.**"

As True Street Media's Twitter account pointed out (alongside many other brilliant barbs aimed at the king's out-of-touch display):

King Charles today said that UK Prime Minister Rishi Sunak's government will "continue to take action...to ease the cost of living for families." King Charles is literally surrounded by gold, wearing a crown of jewels and precious stones, while speaking on costs to help affordability.

There's no way you can slice and dice Charles's current existence to be anything other than "billionaire wears a crown of jewels, takes money from dead subjects for his own enrichment, all while feigning concern for subjects who literally can't afford to keep their electricity on or heat their homes in winter."

But sure, let's attack Meghan for starting her own business with money she earned from working, not from leeching off dead people.

None of this had to come up in a biography about the life and times Meghan and Harry.

Unfortunately, the British media couldn't help themselves. They had to start the jam wars and poke at Meghan for something utterly innocent, and that's what brought scrutiny upon the king, and here we are.

Chapter 14

Cat's in the Cradle

Harry and Meghan would be traveling separately for this one. Harry, nourished and uplifted after celebrating his first-born-son Archie's fifth birthday, went ahead, ignoring taunting headlines about his impending visit to London. There was no way he was going to miss the Invictus Games anniversary service at St. Paul's Cathedral in London.

Once again, Harry was crossing a continent and an ocean to partake in a celebration of life and heroism, and once again the media couldn't handle the wholesome positivity. There are more clicks in hate, and more money in clicks. Ergo, the negativity prevailed.

Instead of focusing on the heroes of Invictus, the tabloids on both shores spun a narrative and fed it all day every day, like a hungry beast.

The early through-line was that King Charles would *not* take the time to see his son while he was in town, even though the son would only be a couple of miles away.

Everyone wanted to know what would happen. *Was this true?* The speculation ratcheted up with every passing day.

Wrote a Page Six reporter, "Harry had been reaching out for over a month to organize a meet-up with his cancer-stricken dad..."

Harry himself was left to quell the speculation. His team released a statement explaining there would be no reunion between father and son. "It unfortunately will not be possible due to His Majesty's full programme. The Duke of course is understanding of his father's diary of commitments and various other priorities and hopes to see him soon."

Upon the release of this news, royal experts and "sources" lined up to opine about what likely went on behind the scenes. Historian and longtime pal of the British royal family Hugo Vickers, for his part, didn't give the king a clean getaway.

"If the king wanted to see Harry, he would find time very easily," Vickers said. "You can never be too busy to see your son."

Indeed. The historian went on to say, basically, *Mate, throw the kid a bone. Have him over for some kippers and Earl Grey. You KNOW you have the time.*

The New York *Post* put it this way: "Vickers said there would be points in the king's diary that he could open up for his youngest son, including breakfast."

You gotta see it Charles's way, though. Why spend time with his irreplaceable second son when instead he could take meetings with lame duck Prime Minister Rishi Sunak, who would be out of office months later, and also attend a tea-and-crumpets party at Buckingham Palace, which is literally down the road from Harry's event?

In all seriousness, the king faced a surprising backlash for his perceived pettiness, even from supposed friends and courtiers.

Charles, one former courtier said, "is not going to throw the weight of the institution behind Invictus again...This all seems very logical inside the palace bubble, but the trouble is that people who don't particularly care about such things, who are dimly aware that the royals spend their days visiting community centers and opening supermarkets, are going to wonder why they are boycotting this terrific charity that is headed by the king's son."

This, Tom Sykes wrote in the *Daily Beast*, is another example of the royal institution's propensity to cut off its nose to spite its face. This, as readers of the *Harry & Meghan* biography series know, is a habit they can't seem to shake. The bubble is too insulated by design, and they have no desire to break out of it, so their missteps continue apace. Charles is too busy cosplaying Henry VIII and finding more expensive cars to carry his crown in to step back and seek insight into his own behavior and baggage.

To illustrate what King Charles the Cruel was doing to his son, the world's media produced copycat headlines that week, all of them with some version of the word "snub" in it. Snubbed, snubbing, snubalicious, snubtastic. Say it ten times fast and it loses all meaning. Anyway…

Kingy-poo made the Buckingham Palace garden party mandatory for working royal family members, even though it was thrown during the Invictus service down the lane, according to royal experts.

"King Charles ordered all working royals (including Princess Anne and Prince Edward, and excluding Prince William and Kate Middleton) to attend a garden party for 5,000 people at Buckingham Palace taking place at the same time," Tom Sykes wrote in the *Daily Beast*.

And so it happened that Prince Harry, head held high, was the only royal to roll up to the Invictus Games anniversary service at St. Paul's Cathedral in London on May 8.

The reality was a joyful, uplifting moment. Harry stepped out of his Rover, trusty bodyguard Chris Sanchez, aka "King of the Back Exits," by his side along with Met officers in yellow vests, to cheers and heartfelt cries of "We love you, Harry! Wooooo!"

Harry glowed. This was part of his family, too, and it was enough.

Though royals weren't there, his close family was. How is that, you ask? The Spencers! They flooded the pews to support their favorite nephew, cousin, grand-nephew, as Harry's genuine efforts to make the world a better place gave them solace as they saw Princess Diana reflected in his eyes and his actions.

Deep organ music filled the hall as Harry greeted, hugged, smiled, and blew kisses to his Spencer relatives. Actor Damian Lewis recited William Ernest Henley's poem "Invictus," which the prince's organization is named after.

Hanging over the day was the sensitive matter of the older brother or, as some on social media call him, *TOB: The other brother.*

By then, royal sources say, Harry and Prince William had not spoken in a year. The estrangement persisted and the distance widened when, that same day, William led an investiture ceremony at Windsor Castle, which was finished by the time Harry's service began.

Harry's family in England really did it: They ghosted him en masse.

Together again

Meghan, the Duchess of Sussex, freshened up after her marathon flight from LAX, then waited patiently in Heathrow Airport's Windsor VIP suite for her beloved to join her. She had work to do. She never shirked the labor of studying and planning for events, never found herself idle in the run-up to international tours.

Meghan's preparation for appearances throughout her life has been rigorous. This landmark tour in Nigeria would be no different. She was not going to show up in the capital city of Abuja without knowing the customs, fashion, manners and as much history as she could learn.

There would be no flubs or PR disasters akin to the gasp-worthy ones William and Kate allowed to happen on their royal tours, like that time they rode high on thrones carried by Black people, or when they stood smiling as Black people clawed at them from behind fences, or when we saw that upsetting video of Kate flinching and pulling away when a Black woman reached for her to dance.

This would be Harry and Meghan's first official international tour since they moved on from their roles as senior working royals in 2020. They made the decision to make the trip after Nigeria's Chief of Defense Staff personally invited them.

Meghan was particularly fascinated by the idea of visiting this African country after a DNA test showed she was 43% Nigerian, from her mother's side.

Upon their arrival in Abuja, temperatures floated around the mid-nineties, and Meghan wore flowy, crepey linens in neutral colors. She wore her hair up but still felt the heat. The Sussexes kicked off their three-day visit at the Lightway Academy school, a beneficiary of their Archewell foundation that trains young girls affected by conflicts in Nigeria.

Harry and Meghan would also be meeting with wounded soldiers and their families in hopes of helping to boost the morale of the soldiers, including those fighting a 14-year war against Islamic extremists in the country's northeast.

As the Sussexes made that first appearance, the pressing crowds couldn't get enough of them, and the media took the opportunity to produce a juxtaposition of two brothers in pictures, as Prince William was also making public appearances at that time. Starkly contrasting images and video of Harry and elder brother William showed the two at public engagements thousands of miles apart.

There was a lonesome shot of William standing alone and digging in the dirt on an empty parcel of land with an old metal shovel, as part of his visit to Cornwall and the Isles of Scilly.

And there were videos of Meghan and Harry swallowed up by a joyful crowd of welcoming Nigerians dressed in vivid colors.

For once, the *Daily Mail* said exactly what I was thinking:

"They were once inseparable brothers, often laughing and joking together at royal events and bound together by a shared grief over the loss of their mother. But the divergent trajectories on which Princes William and Harry now head were on stark display this week as they carried out a series of very different engagements…

"Harry was afforded a rockstar's welcome in Abuja with his wife Meghan Markle as excited crowds clamoured to take selfies and the military rolled out the red carpet."

I'm not sure if the *Mail* thought they were raising William up somehow or not, but all that article did was reinforce the growing chasm between his old-man billionaire stiffness and Harry's relaxed Prince of the People persona. He is, those who knew both mother and son say, very much like his mother Diana, nicknamed Princess of the People for her generous, down-to-earth authenticity.

One charming moment of the Nigeria trip was on that first day as Harry and Meghan supported Invictus and championed mental health for young people affected by war and fighting. At a mental health summit organized by local non-profit GEANCO, a partner of Archewell, the couple were received by a dancing troupe and a crowd of excited students and teachers.

"We've got to acknowledge those amazing dance moves!" Meghan cheered. "My husband was excited to jump up!"

They visited classrooms, too, where delighted children showed the royal couple the robot cars they'd built. The parents of two young children let slip a few details about their own little ones, Archie and Lilibet, and made sure to let the students know it was okay to not be okay.

"In some cases around the world…there is a stigma when it comes to mental health. Too many people don't want to talk about it," Harry said. "So will you promise to us that after today, no more being scared, no more being unsure of mental health?"

"You see why I'm married to him?" a beaming Meghan said of Harry as the room erupted in cheers. "It is a complete honor to have our first visit to Nigeria be here with all of you. We believe in you. We believe in your future."

Twenty-four hours into the visit, Meghan had learned things you can't find in books. Sometimes true understanding comes after you get a feel for a place, a vibe, and are fully immersed.

"I've very quickly gotten the memo," Meghan laughed at one event, "that I need to wear more color so I can fit in with all of you and your incredible fashion."

She was wearing a bright red dress.

The unkind commentators and out-of-touch tabloids tried to sully the effect of the visit by repeating ad naseum how *They're not working royals, they want to have their cake and eat it too by conducing unauthorized, unofficial "royal" tours (this is false), and by the way Harry's British family would be displeased at best, enraged at worst.* But what Harry and Meghan actually accomplished in Nigeria was as simple as bringing joy to our timeline for at least a little while. Through their colorful, moving visit, we could click on the news or hop on social media and see smiles, love, and fun for a moment instead of agony and mayhem. For even just a moment, our spirit was lifted. That matters.

Wrote the woman behind Twitter/X account Why am I Surprised, "I think the world is starving for HOPE right now in an age of fascism, racism, corruption & bigotry. In walks two charismatic people from very different worlds, committed to doing GOOD & inspiring others to do the same. The world embraces them because we NEED them. We need HOPE."

When that trip was over, before she and Harry would take a breath and celebrate their lives and their union, Meghan said, "It was incredibly memorable and special. That alone is the best souvenir to take with us—all the memories we've made."

So glad we made it

Another successful work trip in their rearview mirrors, it was time for date night. For this, their sixth wedding anniversary celebration, Harry and Meghan retreated to a safe space and invited good friends to join them for a Saturday night outing.

Their favorite steakhouse, Lucky's, had become a familiar local hangout where the royals could have an elegant night out while knowing they wouldn't be hounded, that they'd be cocooned in an upscale environment where they and their robust security team were known to management and locals alike.

This would be a special one. Harry and Meghan had been married six years, and had weathered the worst a new couple could take—from a public who blamed Meghan for everything Harry experienced with his dysfunctional family to his own brother warning him against "rushing in" with the American actress and lifestyle influencer. And of course there were the years of made-up headlines talking about "divorce" and how "Harry would return to the UK on his own one day."

Yet here they were, greeting friends Brian and Tracy Robbins, he the head of Paramount Pictures and she a designer. They ordered a bottle of red wine and broke bread at a restaurant where a veggie burger runs $30, the humble baked potato costs $18.50, and a porterhouse steak adds an eye-watering $213 to your bill.

It was the night before their actual anniversary. The date fell on a Sunday, traditionally a family day for the family of four. Gifts would be exchanged, and as Harry and Meghan always do, they'd come up with thoughtful offerings appropriate for the year.

Depending on your taste and whether you prefer a modern or traditional gift exchange, the sixth year of marriage is either iron or sugar.

Sugar is meant to symbolize the sweet story of how the couple fell hard for each other, along with the richness of everlasting love. Iron, on the other hand, represents the solid strength of your marriage and paves the way for many more years to come.

"They love to do their own take on traditional wedding gifts," a source close to the Sussexes once told *People*. "The first anniversary was paper, and Meghan wrote out the wedding speech and had it framed for him." Prince Harry gave his wife an eternity ring to mark their first year of marriage.

On their second anniversary in 2020, says a friend, "They both gave each other gifts based on cotton. Undoubtedly, it was a very creative and romantic gesture as all their gifts are to one another."

All in all, Meghan and Harry were about as settled, happy and grateful as any two people could be in the weeks leading up to the summer of 2024.

Chapter 15

The Summer of 2024

June was quiet on the Sussex front—as far as the public knew. Some fans bemoaned Harry and Meghan's summer retreat from the spotlight. They weren't seen on vacation, and part of the reason was because much of that time was spent in hardcore work mode.

Very often, the less you see of Harry and Meghan, the harder they're working behind the scenes.

Sometimes they're recharging, but in this case, they were zinging with energy and preparing for Meghan's new brand, American Riviera Orchard, to steam in take the celebrity lifestyle space by storm.

Was it a peaceful time for the Sussexes in between the bustling work of daily living? We didn't know either way, because they were nesting, and they were keeping their plans to themselves.

Prince Harry capped off this biographical year with the rift between him and his British family wider than ever. *People* magazine ran a cover story in the heat of July titled "Harry & Charles: The *Real* Reason They're Not Speaking," and it was made clear from the Sussex camp that relations had gone from chilly to frozen solid.

There was no movement, no thaw.

Those close to Harry said the monarch was no longer taking his son's calls or answering his letters.

"He gets 'unavailable right now,'" a friend of Harry's told the magazine. "His calls go unanswered. He has tried to reach out about the King's health, but those calls go unanswered too."

It is, as I have said before, a Greek tragedy in the making the way a father will so easily cut off a son, even if temporarily, while the son faces threats the king knows all too well. Charles will be briefed daily on safety and current threats floating on the intelligence wires, anything that might signal bad actors are targeting him in any serious way.

Charles will protect himself.

His son and his son's precious children are on their own.

Can you imagine?

Whatever you think of Harry or Meghan, that is both heartbreaking and twisted. Harry was born as a prince inside the fishbowl of arguably the world's most-watched royal family, and that comes with a price tag he didn't ask for.

The loser in the end will be Charles, who will have to live with any consequences from denying protection for his own child and grandchildren.

While palace sources toe the party line and point out that constitutionally, the monarch has no power, anyone who reads about and follows the royals knows this is not the case in practice, whatever the fine print says. The King of England holds sway and influence behind the scenes, and the monarch has long been able to influence which royals get police protection and which don't. Stripped of his Metropolitan Police bodyguards in 2020, Harry has been fighting ever since to reinstate police protection for himself and his family, with no success.

"Harry is frightened and feels the only person who can do anything about it is his father," a royal insider also said to *People*.

This is not the first time we've heard of the fear emanating from the brave and capable prince, who has more than proved his valor by serving in the most dangerous war zones in the world.

He's scared. He's asking his father, the person who ostensibly signed up to protect him from birth onward, for help.

If his father ever did help his son, if he'd open his arms to Harry and offer to keep him safe, "it's 'swords down,'" says Harry's friend, who adds that the prince's greatest hope is for reconciliation.

We generally end these biographies on a celebratory note, on Independence Day, as the Sussex family waves their flags and the children stare in wonder at the spectacle of the parade.

We've followed them on these holidays from Jackson Hole to the town just outside their sprawling Montecito property.

This year, though, the media didn't find them.

This year, the Sussexes were free, out of the public gaze, in a place unknown to anyone outside their small circle. No doubt wherever they were, there was red-white-and-blue, summer popsicles, fireworks, and most important, love.

Just as well they had that private family time, because what was coming in the next year would change everything.

Nothing would ever be the same for Harry and Meghan.

Until next time.

xoCourtney

Made in United States
Cleveland, OH
13 April 2025

16063947R00090